SELF-CARE FOR BLACK WOMEN

7 POWERFUL PRINCIPLES AND PRACTICAL TIPS TO RADICALLY PRIORITIZE YOUR WELLBEING, EMBRACE SELF-HEALING AND OVERCOME THE DAILY STRUGGLES

HELENE A. WAIGO

© **Copyright 2023 – Helene A. Waigo All rights reserved.**

The content contained within this book may not be reproduced, duplicated or transmitted without direct written permission from the author or the publisher.

Under no circumstances will any blame or legal responsibility be held against the publisher, or author, for any damages, reparation, or monetary loss due to the information contained within this book, either directly or indirectly.

Legal Notice:

This book is copyright protected. It is only for personal use. You cannot amend, distribute, sell, use, quote or paraphrase any part, or the content within this book, without the consent of the author or publisher.

Disclaimer Notice:

Please note the information contained within this document is for educational and entertainment purposes only. All effort has been executed to present accurate, up to date, reliable, complete information. No warranties of any kind are declared or implied. Readers acknowledge that the author is not engaged in the rendering of legal, financial, medical or professional advice. The content within this book has been derived from various sources. Please consult a licensed professional before attempting any techniques outlined in this book.

By reading this document, the reader agrees that under no circumstances is the author responsible for any losses, direct or indirect, that are incurred as a result of the use of the information contained within this document, including, but not limited to, errors, omissions, or inaccuracies.

CONTENTS

Introduction	5
1. YOUR JOURNEY TO RADICAL SELF-CARE —AN INTRODUCTION TO PRIORITIZING YOURSELF IN MODERN SOCIETY	9
Defining Radical Self-Care for the Black Woman	11
Self-Care Affirmations to Help You Along the Way	26
2. PHYSICAL WELLNESS—EMPOWERING YOUR BODY	29
Cultural Barriers to Physical Self-Care	31
The Benefits of Physical Self-Care— Everything That You Need to Know	34
Affirmations for Loving Our Bodies	57
3. EMOTIONAL SELF-CARE	59
Why Emotional Self-Care Matters	61
Affirmations to Help You Remember That Joy is Your Birthright	76
4. MENTAL SELF-CARE—HEALING THE HEART AND MIND	79
Unpacking Childhood Trauma	83
Choosing to Heal–This is Why We Do It	88
Positive Affirmations to Help You with Your Healing	95
5. SPIRITUAL SELF-CARE	101
Deconstructing the myths about spiritual self-care	104
Affirmations for Spirituality and Peace	115
6. SOCIAL SELF-CARE	117
Focusing on Community Self-Care	119

Affirmations for Community	130
7. PROFESSIONAL SELF-CARE	133
The Lives of Working Black Women	137
Affirming Your Boundaries	146
8. ENVIRONMENTAL SELF-CARE (SUSTAINING A HEALTHY LIFE AROUND YOU)	149
Beyond The Clutter: Creating an Environment That You Love	152
Affirmations for a Peaceful Environment	156
9. CELEBRATING PROGRESS AND MAKING SELF-CARE A LIFELONG JOURNEY	157
Conclusion	163
About the Author	165
References	167

INTRODUCTION

Hi Sis… how are you?

You don't have to give your answer right now. Think about it for a while. Allow the question to sit there with you. Allow it to roar through the silence that echoes as you dig out that answer far beyond the "I'm okay" or "I'm good" you usually give. This book is going to be your place of safety, where you can share your innermost secrets, emotions, and feelings. All my black sisters are welcome, every part of you. The parts that are okay, along with the ones that are not okay.

Throughout this book, you're going to connect with yourself; by the end, you will reintroduce a better version of yourself to the world again. This place and this time are all for you. The place where you realize that life is happening for you instead of to you. The world needs you just as you are. Forget about those unrealistic standards imposed on

INTRODUCTION

women—especially black women— and start thinking more about who you want to be, the stories you want to create, and the connections you wish to make. Show up just as you are so that when others look at you, they too can realize they can thrive and exist in all their authenticity. As we work through the contents of the book, you'll find all the tools and the resources that you need to help you create a more intentional and fulfilling life within these 7 core principles:

- putting yourself first and incorporating self-care into your daily routine
- loving and celebrating the power of your body through physical self-care
- connecting to and making space for your emotions through emotional and mental self-care
- loving your people and allowing yourself to be loved through social and community self-care
- allowing yourself to think bigger and beyond yourself through spiritual self-care
- forging your identity and setting healthy boundaries in the workplace through professional self-care
- loving this planet and surroundings that you call home through environmental self-care

I am and will always be an advocate for looking out and being there for the people I care about first, but I believe that before I can be any good to those I love, I have to be good to myself first. Why? Because that outer glow is nurtured from the inside. We have to protect our inner crown of beauty. It all starts with how you feel about yourself, how you love yourself, and how intentional you are about making yourself a priority.

As black women, we are taught that we should be selfless and put our children, partners, and family's needs before our own. We leave so little room for ourselves, and that is why we so often find ourselves worn down, running on empty, and feeling hopeless at times, juggling an endless "to-do" list. So I, your sister, your advocate, your mentor, am here to teach you that putting yourself first is not about exploiting others, fending for yourself first, or being neglectful and careless about your relationships. It's a lot more about nursing and tending to yourself like you would a garden; it's about creating a cocoon of love, doing what's best for your health in the long run, and building a relationship with yourself that leaves you glowing because you are mesmerized and in love with the life that you are building.

It starts here. Say these words with me:

Be precious with yourself.

Be patient.

Be compassionate.

Be present.

INTRODUCTION

By the end of this journey together, I can only hope that when I ask you how you're doing, you'll respond from a place of deep honesty. You'll respond from a place of true contentment.

Your best days are ahead of you, so let's do this!

ONE
YOUR JOURNEY TO RADICAL SELF-CARE—AN INTRODUCTION TO PRIORITIZING YOURSELF IN MODERN SOCIETY

Sweet soul, you are sacred—sacred because you are life. Take it easy and cherish every moment of this delicate life. Everything that is within you is blooming.

THE BLACK FEMALE figures and role models I have, had tremendous influence over my life. I inherited their passion, their perseverance, their tenacity, and their faith. They taught me how to be independent, self-sufficient, and not rely too heavily on the help of others. I feel a tremendous sense of pride when I step out into the world, dignified, with my head held high because of all that I learned from them.

However, I've come to realize that this strength that was molded within me from an early age was the very thing that stood between me and that abundant life I desperately yearned for. Strength was the armor that I wore to cover up most of my insecurities. It hid away the intense emotions that were bubbling up from the inside. Ironically enough, it held me back and kept me from declaring the boldness of my own truths. This strength lied to and deceived me; it forced me to endure and tolerate things that were harmful to me and my well-being because *I am a black woman, and therefore should be the rock or pillar to everyone around me.* But this strength is the very thing that tore me down, the very thing that broke me because I do not need anybody. With *'I'm fine'* and *'I got this'* attitude. Doesn't this feel and sound a little familiar to you?

I want us to thrive, not merely survive, and the only way we can achieve that is by embracing our brokenness as much as we do our wholeness. Now that, dear sister, is what unshakeable strength is.

DEFINING RADICAL SELF-CARE FOR THE BLACK WOMAN

Self-care is a little concept that we read a little too much about nowadays. Instagram and Pinterest aesthetics paint it as luxury bubble baths, hot chocolates, and manicures on a rainy day, but I want us to sit and think a little bit more about what it actually means for us as black women; the women who were told that we don't deserve that kind of luxury for ourselves; the women who saw our mothers and grandmothers work without a day of rest; the women who were taught we are the sole providers for our families and must work until we are on our deathbeds—the women who were never taught that putting ourselves first is completely okay. Well, I'm gonna start right here and break it down for y'all: radical self-care is letting go of all of those limiting beliefs that we feed ourselves. It's about liberating yourself from the past that has been holding you prisoner for years. It's about teaching yourself to welcome all of your triggers without judgment or shame, getting to know them better, and responding to them from a place of compassion and love. It's about honoring and carrying the fullness of who you are. Being intentional about putting your wellbeing first rather than appeasing to others.

As black women, we have normalized the idea that we have to suffer first before goodness and blessings can find their way to us. We believe that we can't have things just because we deserve them; for us, vulnerability, gentleness, and tenderness are mostly seen as a luxury, instead of an essential emotional need. We need self-care more than most, and there are so many reasons why.

Why Self-Care is Essential for Us as Black Women

Self-care is a practice that can help us find peace when the world is at war with our race and our identity. There's always something about us that the world at large has an issue with. If it's not the loudness of our kinky hair, it's the length of our braids—or it's our bodies—they're too provocative, our skin is dark or too light, we're too loud, we're too angry. Our presence can sometimes have people shifting uncomfortably. Self-care is how we silence all those voices of hate. It's choosing to preserve the sanctity of what lies within our hearts; it's choosing to put ourselves, our health, our joy, and our dreams first in a society that tells us to dim our light and simply get on with it, as we can't change anything. But one thing we need to start changing is how we care for ourselves.

Self-care is a practice that can help us carry the fullness of our emotions. Sis, you have permission to express, feel, and live in your full range of emotions. You are allowed to voice your deepest desires—your fears, your needs, your hopes, your dreams, your loneliness, your sadness—without feeling ashamed about it. You don't have to put up a brave face all the time.

You don't always have to be the "accommodating" one. When we fail to acknowledge the existence of our other emotions, our brains automatically go into a fight or flight mode. Those emotions are going to simmer there within us. Ferment. Manifest and take over. That's going to take a toll on our relationships and our health in general. If we don't welcome those feelings like they want to be welcomed, they will force themselves in, and when that happens, it won't be a pretty sight.

You get to learn what it is that you truly want. The people-pleaser in me does things for people because I tend to think that I cannot be loved, valued, and accepted just as I am, even if I don't have that much to give. In these instances, what do we do? We let other people ride shotgun in our own lives because we think we have to. We choose a career path that pleases our parents or accommodates family circumstances, sometimes sacrificing our one true passion. We change certain things about ourselves because we think that is what society expects of us. Self-care is what helps us grow the language, the strength, and the will to steer our lives in the direction that we want them. It's what allows us to be moved by *our own* choices. When we let go of the idea that acceptance needs certain T's & C's attached to it, we give ourselves the courage and permission to try and go after life relentlessly simply because we can.

Self-care is important because you matter. Sis, you are a gift to this earth. Your existence carries weight. There are people who look at you and think: *This black woman is divine. She is pure light, and I am so glad to have them in my life*. So don't you dare think, even for the briefest of moments, that you mean so little. I've had so many days where I sat up late at night in bed, questioning my worth or asking myself if I did enough during that past day. Did I do enough for my children? What about my work? Or sometimes, I sit there and think to myself, does it really matter? Are there even people who care about me? These are heavy questions, but those self-care practices that I call "love reminders" reinforce how sacred life is. Those emotional check-ins remind me of how far I have come and how far I have yet to go. The amount of running around, late nights, and long hours show how resilient the human body is, and the little love notes that I write to myself remind me of just how free unconditional love is.

To say "I love you" to yourself despite all of your flaws, despite the injustices against you, is a revolutionary act. Your existence deserves to be validated and honored. There's plenty that I could say about the ways and whys of how we should practice self-care, but the why will always remain: the world becomes a slightly better place when I am happy and healthy and when my needs are met.

Self-care is messy. One day it looks like tears. On another day, it looks like unpacking some of your biggest fears or getting out of bed and making it, only to decide to get back underneath the covers again. It's wanting to give up, but putting up a fight and persisting nonetheless. Self-care is living. An act of rebellion. Refusing to entertain any of that debilitating doubt. Choosing to chase that comforting warmth of the sun. It's wrapping yourself up in the beauty of silence and knowing that you are going to be okay.

The Cultural Roots of Self-Care

If you went ahead and did some digging for yourself, you'd find that everybody has their own definition of what self-care looks like. For some, hot tea and a bath will do just the trick. For others it's a full body massage or Spa Day; and others treat themselves to a little Swedish concept called Fika, also known as the sweet art of doing nothing.

But when I look at us as a black community and what we know or how we perceive self-care, I can't help but cry a little inside. The picture that we have come to create (the manicures and pedicures, the bubble baths, chocolates, and pampering oneself with luxury shopping sprees) is generally the westernized version. We are blinded by the fact that our ancestors practiced self-care long before the world developed its obsession with the whole concept. One of the ways through which self-care is rooted in our cultural heritage is through spirituality and maintaining that connection with our ancestors. For our grandmothers and great-grandmothers, spirituality was a symbol of hope, connectedness, and togetherness. Their spirituality gave them something to believe in and a hope to cling to when everything around them seemed hopeless.

African healing practices and African American folklore also played and continue to play a significant role in the lives of many black people. If we take a look at many traditional African healing practices, we learn that they don't just consider the patient and their symptoms, but the holistic picture of their lives, including relationships with friends, family, and their work and home environments. Each of these elements symbolizes and contributes to healing. The symbolism of each of these elements contributes to healing while still honoring that need for a cultural sense of belonging.

Incorporating traditional wellness practices as black women is something that we should consider doing. It is something that can allow us the freedom to discover different approaches to taking control of our well-being. Here are a couple of cultural approaches to wellness that you can consider to help you reconnect with the wisdom of your ancestors:

Earthing. Our ancestors spent the entirety of their lives walking around barefoot. They slept on the ground and did a lot of work requiring contact with the earth using their hands. Earthing is a practice that helps to realign your spirit with the natural rhythms of the earth. The practice involves putting your feet in contact with the bare ground, allowing the purity of earth's energy to restore and revive you back to life. Some of the benefits that this practice can have for you include improved quality of sleep. You'll feel more connected (not just to yourself but to the world around you at large) and much happier too. You can practice grounding by kicking off your shoes and allowing your feet to become one with the grass, the ground, the rocks, or the sand. There are also resources and products that you can purchase that can be used inside your home to create that same feeling and effect.

Herbal healing. In the society that we live in today, convenience is a front-runner when it comes to matters of health and well-being. It's a lot easier to open up the UberEats app and order something from there than it is to spend 40 to 45 minutes preparing a wholesome meal from scratch in your own kitchen. But we are what we consume. So if we spend the majority of our time consuming negative media, we're going to start seeing the after-effects through our anxiety and uneasiness. The same applies to the food that we eat as well. This isn't to say that our ancestors didn't encounter any challenges when it came to making smarter lifestyle choices, but what I would like to point out is that the practices that they developed could teach us a thing or two about natural remedies to help restore the balance within the body, instead of relying too heavily on overly processed modern remedies. There are natural herbs and plants that we can use for our skin and hair to help improve our overall health and, ultimately how we feel about ourselves. I am an advocate for the black natural revolution, and it goes a long way in improving and healing our body, mind, and soul.

Everything That Self-Care Isn't—The Myths

I am sure that there is a lot that you have heard about self-care. The one that I hear often is that self-care is something that is not for black women...And why is that? Because for us, exhaustion is seen as a status symbol. Our mothers and our grandmothers held on to everything and put it on their shoulders and as a rule, we inherited a mentality from them that to prove that we are just as equal as our white counterparts, we would have to work twice as hard. We've gotten used to operating in survival mode, and that is why something such as rest becomes something that we don't allow ourselves to even talk about, but we should. We should be engaging in more conversation about why rest is such a sacred practice. So let's bust those myths about self-care together.

Myth 1: Self-care means you're lazy. Self-care does not equate to laziness or letting that strong black woman image down. Ask yourself this question: what do you do when your phone or laptop battery runs out? You charge your devices. Sister, take off your superwoman cape and gently ease into the sweet rhythm of doing nothing. Luxuriate in that simplicity of doing something, not because you have to, but because you want to, because it brings joy. We are humans, not robots designed to create, produce, or do something all the time. Rest promises renewal to us. With renewal comes more fulfillment and increased vitality for life, and that means you will get to show up for yourself and your people; the things that matter most to you with blazing passion.

So here are a few self-care check-ins that you can hold on to when you don't feel compelled to keep going. Jot them down and recite them daily:

- Rest does not have to be earned.
- No one was made to be productive all the time.
- You can still be good, and show up for all that you need to while being kind to yourself.
- You deserve to give yourself a lot more credit than you are for all that you're doing.

Myth 2: Self-care is a luxury. Hear me out: self-care is not a luxury. It is a necessity and should be ingrained in our daily routines. It is just as essential as the very air that we breathe. We often hear people saying they're going to treat themselves to a slice of cake, a mug of decadent hot chocolate, or a glass or two of wine after a strenuous day because they've earned it. But just as much as self-care is about treating ourselves to life's fine pleasures, we need to acknowledge that it is also about doing the very things that we don't want to be doing. It's opting for the nourishing and nutrient-filled meal because it's the better option for our gut health. It's teaching yourself healthier coping mechanisms to help regulate your emotions. It's saving instead of splurging, having the willingness to alter those citations that we sometimes see as unmanageable:

The key to sustainable and healthy self-care doesn't lie in how much you can spend or splurge. It's more of a matter of learning to settle in and tune in to our hearts to get to the essence of what really is good for us.

Myth 3: Self-care is too time-consuming. It doesn't have to be because it is something that we can easily slip into our daily activities. I am a lover of all things that are nurturers and cultivators of joy. Some days are messier than others, and it is on those days when I need to remind myself that joy exists all around me. All I need to do is look around and pay close enough attention. You don't need to dedicate hours and hours at a time. Self-care can be scheduled into those moments while you're waiting in the checkout line. You can use those couple of minutes to lean into a practice of self-affirmation and gratitude. Speak words that reaffirm your worth. Words that uplift and empower you to show up boldly and audaciously. It can be created during your morning drives to work. If you know that you're going to be stuck in traffic for almost an hour, use that time as your moment for self-reflection. Do some soul work and ask yourself these questions:

- Are you genuinely happy? If your answer is yes, what can you do to continue building on that joy? If it's no, what areas in your life do you think you could change? What things can be done differently?

- What are you most proud of? What are your biggest accomplishments over the days that have passed?
- What did you do yesterday or today that you couldn't have imagined yourself doing a couple of months or years back?
- Are you showing up for yourself with kindness, compassion, and grace?
- Are you working on healing your inner child? If you could say anything to them right now, what would you say to them?

Make sure to reflect on each question and answer them honestly, use a post-it-note and keep them in your car.

Myth 4: Self-care is something that doesn't require consistent practice. No, self-care is not a one-time event. Self-care is an ongoing process that requires you to show up consistently on the good days, the bad ones, and the in-betweeners. It's a lot like the healing process that you have to unpack gradually. It is layered and complex. You discover various things about yourself throughout the process; things that you like and things that you don't necessarily like. And in the middle of that, you'll have to explore and dig deeper into what those things mean to you, which is something that will not happen in one day. It's about giving yourself the time and patience that you need to explore the avenues of your life that you must.

Myth 5: Self-care is about perfection. Self-care wants us in the middle of our mess. *"Self-care is something I will start practicing when…"* It hurts me when I hear women say something like that. Like, why not now? When you're practicing self-care, you're not in competition with anybody else, so all that is required of you is to show up as you are. Self-care wants you with that broken heart and the tears in your eyes. It wants you with all your doubts and hesitations, because it wants to help you figure it all out. The messy middle—that's where it wants you—is that place where things are confusing, difficult, or don't make all that much sense. So stop waiting on the perfect moment to have it all figured out or for the ideal circumstance. Come as you are and load off all that you need to; it is that safe space for you to show your vulnerabilities and authenticity.

Myth 6: Self-care should look the same for everyone. Nope. Our needs are different, so that means that our requirements for self care are going to look a lot different from one another as well. Self-care is about working on different areas of our lives at any particular time. Our physical and emotional needs differ, and we also deal with emotional hardships differently. Someone may de-stress by going out for a walk; someone else may opt to go for a run instead, while someone else may choose to meditate. It's not a one-size-fits-all kind of approach. You get to and should define what it means for you.

Myth 7: Self-care is about making a choice between you and others. As much as it's about distancing ourselves from people and situations that aren't good for us, it's also about strengthening those existing relationships and bonds that light us up from the inside out and keeping ourselves in check so that we aren't consumed by our toxic behaviors. One of the hardest things for me to do sometimes is to admit that I was in the wrong or that my actions were the root cause of someone else's grief or pain. Sometimes we are the toxic ones, and engaging in self-care practices encourages regular reflection so that we don't make a habit of those toxic behaviors. No soul is a perfect one, but what matters most is the quest for continuous self-improvement. Doing the inner work by weeding through and plucking out those weeds that deter our blooming process.

Myth 8: Self-care is the solution to all of our mental health struggles. As much as I wish that this was true, I have to step up and say that it is not a medical cure. It is in many ways beneficial and has many wonderful and positive effects on our mental health, but we cannot treat it as the solution to everything because self-care practiced mindlessly can have dire consequences for our overall wellness in general. It is about meeting yourself at the most realistic place possible and being discerning enough about when it might be time to ask for help from a professional.

Myth 9: Self-care is only about our mental health. Our lives are an oasis of experiences. We experience and go through multiple things that make us who we are. There are physical, spiritual, social, and emotional elements involved. Loving and caring for yourself means taking into account all of those factors.

Run to that place that is love, and if that place is with you, then by all means, please spend some time there. There is nothing in this world as beautiful and as divine as getting to know yourself on a deeper level. Celebrate and nurture that relationship that you are building with yourself. Guard and trust in that beautiful heart of yours. And if you ever need a reminder or that word of wisdom, here are my **top ten self-care reminders** that you can rest your head on; on the days when you feel weary and tired:

❀ Self-care is about things that are meaningful, worthwhile, and necessary for our progression, even if they may not initially feel all that good.

❀ It's going to be a challenging and difficult process on certain occasions because it's going to require you to face and challenge yourself instead of running away from your fears. It's about admitting that maybe you don't like yourself all that much where you currently are and that you're going to do the very best that you can to move closer to the truth of who you want to be.

❀ You are in full control of your life. You don't have to wait on anybody to tell you that it's okay for you to start practicing self-care or doing things for your wellbeing and mental health. Do it for you because you deserve them.

❋ Self-care is also life's way of allowing us to enjoy life where we are exactly as we should. You may not be where you want to be, or it may feel like your life has just become stagnant with a lack of progress, but remember that you are not where you used to be, and that in itself is a sign of progress.

❋ Accepting your needs in all their uniqueness is how you tap into that well of authenticity. When you dig deep, your heart knows what you want and need. So, look within for all your self-care inspiration. Your heart knows what you need and will never lie to you.

❋ Remember that it takes effort. If you don't put in the necessary work that needs to be done, then you are not going to get the transformation that you need. It is not enough to merely wish for one. You have to wake up each day with the intention to do the work that needs to be done, regardless of how difficult, painful, or messy the process may be.

❋ Honesty is required because without it, you will not be able to move forward toward progress. Sometimes, you'll fall back and have to start all over again. In those moments, remind yourself over and over that you are not a failure, but you are a person 'In Progress' and are finally learning that things *can* actually get better.

❋ You may need to let go of people, places, and things to be able to love yourself a little bit louder. So don't resist that change that is meant to happen because you're trying to carry everything and everyone into the next chapter. Spread those wings and permit yourself to fly.

✻ Good things are all around you in abundance. The beauty of this work is boundless, and there's happiness all around and available for your taking. Reach out and grab it.

✻ Life is far too precious to spend on things that deplete and drain us of our energy. So spend your energy on things and people that pour energy back into you.

Sister, I hope you find the courage to choose yourself over and over and over again. That you opt for growth over comfort or convenience; that you fight for the peace and unbridled joy that you do deserve. You deserve all the love and blessing that this world has to offer.

SELF-CARE AFFIRMATIONS TO HELP YOU ALONG THE WAY

I will be kind to myself by adorning myself with the care and love that I need.

There is only one of me that exists, so I must ensure that I remain good and true to myself.

Putting care into how I am taking care of myself is how I am able to take care of others.

Love is the root of all self-respect. So, therefore right here, right now, I am choosing to say: I love myself.

I am worthy of living an extraordinary life.

All parts of me are equally beautiful. The darkness and the light alike. Self-care is how I can teach myself to exist with all of these parts together.

I am slowing down. Using less force and embracing more flow because the best parts of life are right there, in the middle of stillness.

Time is fleeting, and my energy is sacred. I will not deny myself the chance to rest fully.

TWO
PHYSICAL WELLNESS—EMPOWERING YOUR BODY

Dear Body, I whisper,

Thank you for being so good to me even through those times when I am not good to you. Thank you for allowing me to live through you.

MOVEMENT MAKES ME FEEL ALIVE. When I engage in these activities, they remind me of what a blessing it is to have a body that can do a million things.

I want to help you understand that physical wellness is not just all about losing weight; it's much deeper than that.

So let me break it down for you.

It's about learning and teaching yourself to cultivate a healthy relationship with your body. Diet culture and the media have warped our perception with unrealistic expectations about what the ideal female body should look like. As black women, we are built differently, and we have to understand that not all of us can be a size zero or even desire to be one. There are people out there who simply aren't willing to understand or become curious about body diversity. This isn't because they're not intelligent enough but because there aren't enough conversations going around to help them challenge their narratives. Embracing and defining physical self-care is our opportunity to embrace, love, and honor our voluptuous bodies while ensuring that we do the necessary work to ensure that our bodies continue to serve us as well as they do.

It's not only about food but about learning to cultivate a healthier relationship with food. Incorporating foods that are nourishing and foods that we enjoy. Foods that help us embrace our cultural heritage. There's so much circling on the internet about what it is that we should and should not be eating. Some of those messages make us believe that we should be ashamed of our cultural foods.

It's about restoring that connection with our bodies and becoming one with it. We pour so much of our energy into other people and other commitments. So to restore that balance, we have to find ways to pour back into ourselves so that we don't leave ourselves running on empty. Burnout, exhaustion, and fatigue are some of the implications that come when we don't refill our reservoir of energy.

It's about helping you maintain that body-mind connection. When we are unwell and feel uneasiness in our bodies, we tend to make decisions that aren't so wise.

So by preserving your physical health, you are preserving the state of your mind.

Lastly, it can be fun! So many of us have had a negative relationship or experience with physical self-care because we're told that if it's not in the gym, then it doesn't count. But the best way to actually build a positive relationship with movement is to make it fun for yourself; that way, you're more likely to be engaged in the process and more motivated to make it part of your routine.

CULTURAL BARRIERS TO PHYSICAL SELF-CARE

A couple of years ago, I was talking to an acquaintance, and the topic of exercise just so happened to worm its way into the conversation. Having seen firsthand what the benefits of being more active can do for you, I naturally wanted to share some of that excitement with her, hoping she would make the same lifestyle changes to improve her quality of life. Instead, I was met with an answer that shattered my heart. She told me that she doesn't exercise because of her hair. "Imagine—mid-workout—my hair looking all wild, frazzled, and unkempt. I don't want anybody out here thinkin' I'm a crazy. Plus I can't wash it this week I've just got it done" So if she felt like this, surely there were plenty other black women, who may have felt the same way.

Achieving society's so-called aesthetic with straight hair is not something that is easy, especially for us black women. The trauma that our hair has to endure—from a silk press, or harsh chemical relaxers and damaging heat, is a nightmare. We're better off loving the texture in its natural form. No one tells a leopard that its spots are uneven in size, so it should do something about them, or it should shed layers and layers of its skin to get rid of them. The same analogy should apply to us and our hair as well. We shouldn't let these barriers stop us from achieving our physical goals.

Physical wellness isn't always all that simple when it comes to black women. Some of the health risks we are more predisposed to include high blood pressure, fibroids, type 2 diabetes with higher risks within pregnancy and labor. So we, more than most, need to be pushing for physical care, as it's vital for our bodies. We should take more ownership simply by checking our own breasts, monitoring our periods, as we can easily be left behind and neglected in this health arena as the world doesn't want to know, learn or fund research about our physical barriers. Therefore it's important to seek medical advice, get regular medical check-ups, and screenings to help detect and prevent health issues early on. If possible, a black doctor can be of more help, as they are more likely to understand the health challenges we face.

Another issue is that most people look at black women's bodies and automatically assume that we don't take care of our bodies or exercise because we are naturally much curvier; we have fuller figures. But we need to start changing the narrative of "size" being the only health determinant. Health has no size. Health is about being able and capable with your body. Being able to do things. It's about being strong and able to live life to your fullest without any limitations.

Food is also a love language in black households and communities. It's how we show one another that we care. It's how we connect with those who are closest to us. It is more than just a means of survival—it is a symbol of our identity, so a lot of women tend to think that making certain changes to their diet may mean neglecting their cultural identity, but I want to tell you right here and now that it doesn't have to be the case. Your food and food traditions can be part of the lifestyle that you are building. You don't have to leave any part of yourself behind.

THE BENEFITS OF PHYSICAL SELF-CARE—EVERYTHING THAT YOU NEED TO KNOW

I love to move my body. Running, dancing, walking, jumping rope—pretty much anything that allows me to celebrate my able limbs. One study that was conducted determined that it is because African-Americans carry a gene that makes us more sensitive to salt, hence the reason why we're more at risk of high blood pressure and heart disease. We need to understand how our bodies work specifically for us black women to inform us what physical movements will best benefit our genetic makeup.

Let's jump right into how movement can benefit us in our lives.

Improved body awareness. Life can get pretty crazy at times, and what most of us do when things get too busy is hit autopilot and start to live fully in our heads. That is why so many of us are out of touch with our bodies. What we all really need is to be able to point out at any given time what our bodies need and to honor that request. This awareness is what helps us remain anchored in the present moment because by checking in with our bodies, we bring better self-awareness and self-guidance to life's challenges.

Poor health habits ultimately contribute to your stress levels. There's something about that body-mind connection that enables you to resort to healthier coping mechanisms. Before I started taking an active approach to take care of my physical health, I would always resort to unhealthy coping mechanisms to deal with the things that were stressing me out, but instead of making me feel any better, I always found myself feeling worse than I initially did, and then have to work twice as hard to get rid of that stress. The health challenges that come with having to deal with all of that stress will directly influence other areas of your life as well (i.e., regular tasks are going to be all the more difficult for you to do. It may affect your financial health as well interfere with your ability to earn a living for yourself).

This is How You Do It—Taking Care of Your Body

If you take care of your body, your body will reward you by taking care of you. There are 5 pillars of physical self-care that we, as black women, should cover when looking to improve our physical well-being. Those include our **nutrition, our movement, our skin, our sleep routines, and our hair.** All five of those pillars need to be addressed to ensure that you create a healthy life for yourself.

But don't worry I've got you covered when it comes to that. We'll have a look at the approaches that can help us navigate those 5 pillars.

Our Nutrition

I know what you might be thinking here; I'm going to tell you to start living off of green juices, celery, and kale. Not a chance–changing our normal habits takes time, and that is why I'm here, so we can work towards adapting some of those bad habits. So we can start to feel good from the inside, so it's not about setting unrealistic goals. Nutrition is as much about the benefits as it is about enjoyment. You don't have to deprive yourself of the foods that you have loved your entire life because they don't fit into a healthy lifestyle. All foods fit. It's simply a matter of mindfulness and moderation.

Here are some simple tips to get you started on the right track.

- Turning the television, your computer, or phone off when it's meal-time
- Taking breaths or pauses in between bites of food
- Chewing, savoring, and relishing in every bite of food
- Keeping your feet firmly to the ground (i.e., having your dinner at the table instead of in bed or on the couch.

Don't go grocery shopping without a list. Have an action plan because if you don't, you may just be tempted to buy everything that looks good or is on sale. Take some time and map out the meals that you want to have for the week or the next couple of days (this will also give you an idea of the quantities you should buy, which means less wastage as well). Plus, you get to look up healthier meal options that you alone or the whole family can enjoy. We all get into a habit of cooking the same meals week after week, me included, so start creating healthier new meal options. A little pre-planning will go a long way, nutrition-wise.

Bake or roast your foods instead of deep frying them. The preparation method for food matters, just as much as what you are actually eating. Baking or roasting (slow cooking, stewing, broiling, poaching, and air frying included) require less oil which makes it better for your heart health, but I am not saying that you should stay completely away from deep frying your foods. You're allowed to indulge every now and again in a tasty deep-fried dish because it's delicious, but moderation is the keyword!

Don't forget to hydrate. If I am being honest with y'all, I'd have to admit that I do not drink as much water as I should be drinking because I would much rather be sipping on a cocktail than an unflavored glass of liquid. However, that cocktail certainly does not have as many benefits as water, but luckily for you, if you're just like me, I've learned that there are a variety of sneaky ways through which you can bump up your aqua intake for the day.

❀ **You eat it.** Hydrate with fruits or veggies that are water-packed. These are fruits and veggies such as watermelons, cucumbers, tomatoes, and zucchini.

❀ **Flavor your water.** If it's the bland taste of water that typically puts you off, chop up some strawberries, lemon slices, berries, cucumbers, or whatever fruit tickles your fancy and add that to your water for an extra burst of flavor. Look around in your local grocery store as well for natural citrus flavors that you can add to your water.

❀ **Keep a water bottle with you** when you go out to remind yourself that you still have water that you need to drink. So many of us don't actually drink water because we simply don't keep our botttles nearby and in sight. So, when you go to the gym, keep it with you. Keep one too on your desk or on the counter in the kitchen, or bedroom.

❀ **Use an app as your accountability partner.** Being aware of whether or not you're meeting your daily intake will be motivation enough to move closer toward your progress. An application called 'Daily Water' can be downloaded on your smartphone, and the best part about it is that you'll get notification pings throughout the day to alert you where your intake for the day currently lies. It's done wonders for me.

Focus more on eating whole-grain foods. Whole grains have a much higher fiber intake than refined carbohydrates, which makes them excellent for your gut health. Foods that are higher in fiber are also more satisfying (so you eat less of them but still feel satisfied after eating). Besides that, these foods contain vitamins, minerals, and a variety of nutrients that puts you at a lower risk of developing diabetes and heart disease. Here's a list of foods that are high in fiber that you should consider incorporating more of into your diet:

- oats
- brown rice
- whole wheat bread
- popcorn (you don't only have to wait for movie nights)
- chia seeds
- dark chocolate (I bet you weren't expecting to see chocolate on the list!)
- nuts
- apples
- beans

Incorporate tons of fruits and vegetables into your lifestyle. The nutritional benefits are typically the same, fresh or frozen and even canned, so you don't have to feel ashamed about opting for the canned or frozen versions. Listen, you don't only have to steam your vegetables for them to be tasty.

Here's what I typically do to make eating veggies easier for my family and me:

✿ **Make your own dips and chutneys.** Hummus is such a great way to sneak in extra veggies. You use chickpeas and can add other vegetables as well to flavor it as well such as roasted carrots or tomatoes. You can use it as a spread for your bread, as a dip for veggie slices, or eat it together with crackers.

✿ **Blend and make smoothies.** A well-made smoothie tastes just as good as a milkshake does! There really are no rules or limits when making smoothies. Throw together your favorite selection of fruits and veggies (bananas and berries are typically my go-to's) and some yogurt, and you've got a nutrient-packed, delicious on-the-go snack.

✿ **Blend them into your sauces.** If you're making a pasta dish, you can always add more veggies to your tomato-based sauce to increase its nutritional value.

✿ **Have no-meat or vegetarian weekdays.** There is so much that you can do: make burger patties from beans or lentils, and have days of the week dedicated to different kinds of vegetable curries or soup. These nights will also encourage you to be more creative around the kitchen. You can also involve the kids or the whole family to make it fun for everyone.

✿ **Snack away.** Apples and peanut butter. Carrots or baked veggies with your hummus dip. Dried fruits are also a great option, but be mindful of the ones that have a bunch of added sugars and artificial flavorings.

Intermittent Fasting, also growing in popularity is another eating plan to incorporate into your lifestyle. You choose a specific time of the day to eat or reduce how many meals you eat in a day. It is very dependent on what eating schedules you choose for yourself, as there are different approaches. Its all about being mindful and strict about what you consume and when. It may not be for everyone, but it's a great option to look into as it has great health benefits, but I suggest only adopting this method for the short term, as it has different effects on different people, and there will be a period of adjustment before your body becomes accustomed to the fasting.

Movement

Movement is all about enjoyment. You shouldn't be punished for what you ate or because diet culture says that your body's form needs to change. Think about it this way: if you tell yourself that you have to go for that run or to the gym because you had a donut or something that you were not supposed to eat, you're going to end up hating exercise —literally. Learning to move your body in ways you enjoy is as beneficial to your mental health as it is to your physical health. I call this *'joyful movement,'* and these are a few of my favorite for you:

Change your script about movement. The messages that surround us tell us that fit bodies mean abs, toned legs, thighs, and upper arms. The problem is that those messages are more focused on aesthetic results. There are a lot more benefits to movement. So if exercise was only ever a punishment for foods you ate or something that you did to change your body, start thinking of it as a tool that will help you get the most and best out of life. You'll be able to keep up with your kids when they ask you to play outside with them. You'll be more alert, have more energy, feel happier, and be more relaxed in general.

Find people or places where your heart and soul feel more at ease. If exercise is something that you never truly engaged in, then a new gym or exercise environment will make you feel out of place. Being in a positive, supportive, and non-judgmental environment will help you feel more confident in your skin and at ease when trying workouts that are a physical challenge.

Lean into your strengths. What are you good at? If you're an excellent dancer, you can consider taking dance classes instead of opting for a traditional gym environment. So start with the things that feel most familiar, and once you've finally tapped into your rhythm, you can gradually challenge yourself to try activities that are out of your comfort zone.

Making Movement a Part of Your Everyday Routine

The great thing about movement is that it doesn't have to be overly complicated or complex. The fitness pages on Instagram tend to make us think that the activity we do doesn't count if we're not running miles and miles an hour or if we aren't spending hours at a time in the gym, but it's not about that at all.

I want you to remember that even if you don't have that 45-minute window to squeeze in a workout in the morning, you can still break up your daily movement goals into smaller bits.

So here are 5 useful strategies you can do to incorporate more movement into your day.

1) Park further away from the entrance when you go to the grocery store. I know what you might be thinking, that you're going shopping, so you want your car to be as near to the entrance as possible to make it more convenient for you, but parking further away means you'll have to walk a greater distance to get to the entrance and that means more steps for you.

2) If you have a sedentary office job or if you work from home, take a 10-minute stretch every hour and a half or so. Moving your body during these breaks will give you a bit more energy when it's time to get back into your work again. Also prioritize desk exercises. having a desk job does not mean that you have to be sedentary. Keep some mini dumbbells in your drawer and do some bicep curls while making telephone calls or scrolling through your emails.

3) Get your earphones out, put your favorite music on, and dance in the kitchen. Find an excuse to make some healthy snacks. Why? Because when you're in the kitchen, you move around a lot, so that means that you're naturally getting in more movement throughout your day. Plus, we just love our music. Its joy to the soul. Whether it's old skool '70s to '80s blues or modern RnB beats, shake a leg and move those hips. You can turn it into a solo dance party. Even incorporate some lunges or squats.

4) Use the house as a work out space, get walking up and down those stairs, no matter how small or big the space. You can walk miles in and around your own home. To make it more interesting you can get on the phone to a friend, while you walk lets call it *'walk & talk'* and then you won't even realise the amount of additional steps and movements you are adding to your day.

5) Involve your family and friends. Movement is fun when we engage in it with other people. Ask your kids if they want to join you on your walk, or instead of your usual coffee or lunch dates with a friend, suggest yoga or a dance class. Or you can still make the coffee, but make it a walking coffee date where you explore the neighborhood and its offerings.

Sleep

A good night's rest is just as important as meeting your daily activity count.

Here's why it matters…..

More sleep means that you'll be in an even better mood. Do you ever wonder why you wake up feeling grouchy and irritated in the mornings? That's because you're not getting the quality of sleep that you should be. Sleep is restorative for the body. It helps boost your energy levels. That's why getting it in sufficient quantities makes you a happier, friendlier person to be around. Also, it is important to take note that not getting enough sleep can lead to severe anxiety and, in the worst-case scenario, depression!

Better mental health. Lack of sleep negatively impacts our ability to think coherently, learn, or function at our best, and keep our memories. When we sleep, our brains update the connections that help us retain and absorb new information better. Essentially when you're well-rested, you'll be more inclined to make better decisions. In other words, you're going to be more productive.

A lack of sleep causes weight fluctuations. I don't know about you, but my appetite changes drastically depending on how much sleep I get. This is because too little rest causes our stomachs to produce more of that hunger hormone called ghrelin—that's what gives our tummies the cues to seek out more food. So less sleep equals frequent snacking, which means more calories and thus weight gain. So getting adequate sleep will ensure that you remain well in sync with your hunger-fullness cues.

Building a Sleep Routine: Tips to Help You Sleep Better

I sometimes wish that falling asleep were as simple as just climbing into bed, closing your eyes, and letting your body do the rest of the work, but it doesn't work like that. It's a process that requires a ton of work, consistency, and commitment. So, where does one even start?

Commit to a schedule. When you're working on an important deadline for work, or when you want to squeeze in a coffee date with the girls, what do you do? You adjust your schedule slightly so that you are able to accommodate those time commitments. It should work the same with your sleep schedule as with yourself. Treat it as a special date with yourself that you simply cannot miss out on. Creating that habit of going to bed and waking up at the same time will help your body adjust, and it will be a lot easier for you to fall asleep as well in the evenings.

Tone down on the electronics and negativity before bedtime. Look, I won't lie. There's nothing I like more than scrolling mindlessly through TikTok or Instagram just before my bedtime—throw in a little bit of Netflix there in the background as well—but in all honesty, the blue light coming from those devices is what's coming in between us and our much-needed "zzz's". Putting those electronics away and silencing social media gives our bodies enough time to adjust and to activate sleep mode. Its also not healthy for our emotional state as it can sometimes put you in a the wrong mindset before bed which can easily sit, and fester with you, as you sleep. Even watching too much TV, reporting on negative news and constant race-related media as well as black trauma movies are also contributing factors.

Try to have dinner much earlier. That chocolate chip cookie or creamy serving of pasta is without a doubt delicious, but reality check, it's not doing you any favors when it comes to helping you with sleep. Having food and drinks before bed triggers indigestion. Ensuring that you eat at least 2 hours before bedtime will ensure that your body processes the food well without disrupting your sleep cycle.

Slow down and settle before bed. In other words, romanticize those hours leading up to your bedtime. What do I mean by that? Pamper yourself. By pampering, I am not referring to extravagant and time-consuming routines; I am merely saying that you should make your evenings more beautiful by doing activities that you love, activities that remind you of the sanctity of rest. If you're a lover of tea, brew yourself a cup before bed, and enjoy a book or a podcast while you sip on it. Take a long, slow shower and allow the exhaustion of the day to wash off.

A few of my favorite tips to help create a peaceful sleeping environment for yourself include:

Make your bed up in the morning before you leave your house for work. Your bed has to have an inviting place to come to each night.

Investing in some good linen or a pair of new soft, quality pajamas. These items will help make going to bed feel more like a pleasure and something to look forward to, rather than something that just happens when you're exhausted. Enjoy the time leading up to bedtime.

Make your bedroom environment a more peaceful one by incorporating some of these things (the bonus is you don't really have to break your bank account; most of these ideas mentioned are rather budget-friendly):

✱ **Invest in a proper mattress.** It can be hard to sleep if your mattress doesn't provide the support it needs. The best types to choose from are memory foam mattresses because they are made from a material that molds the shape of your body, which is perfect for helping to correct your posture and providing relief from back pain.

✱ **Incorporate some greenery to make you feel close to nature.** You don't have to go out and buy a whole plant nursery, but you should consider ones that release oxygen throughout the night as you sleep: English ivy, orchids, aloe vera, peace lilies, or rubber plants, to name a few.

* **Keep it minimal and clutter-free**. Clutter impacts our overall ability to think coherently. Declutter your environment and get rid of anything that is not supposed to be in the bedroom. That is the best way to create a positive environment that will make it much easier for you to relax.

* **Aroma therapy for the win**. Make your space smell as pleasant as possible. Buying some candles always does the trick for me. Keep them on your dresser or bedside table.

* **Keep the lighting as atmospheric as possible**. You want to keep away from the harsh light as much as possible. Dimmer, lower light helps make the brain feel more at ease and will allow you to drift a little further into your state of relaxation.

* **Keep your walls as simple as possible**. Just as you would a table, you don't really want your walls to be cluttered with stuff. So choose a side of your bedroom wall to serve as the focal point. That way, there'll be less mental clutter. You can also get a black art picture and hang it up in your bedroom, one that resembles tranquility or something you connect with.

* **Do a bedtime body scan**. Climb into bed and lie on your bed with your arms outstretched and legs comfortable apart from one another. Ensure that you feel cozy and warm enough because if the conditions aren't ideal for you, it may create some issues in helping you relax. Inhale deeply for about four seconds, and when you're ready, allow yourself to exhale slowly. Repeat this about three to

four times until you can feel the tension fall all the way into your bed. Allow your legs to soften and your arms and belly to soften too. Allow any tension that you feel in your neck, shoulders, and back to soften and as well. Soften your lips and allow your jaw to soften. As you do that, you might feel your eyes and your brain starting to relax. Thank your body for carrying through this practice and for everything else that it does for you, and allow yourself to sink into a blissful state of sleep.

Your Skin

Your skin glimmers and catches the attention of pacers when you walk by in public. *"Look at me,"* it says. *"You cannot deny the boldness of my existence."*

Sis, these words right here are an invitation for you to glorify the blackness of your skin—whatever shade of black it is wrapped in. Love it. Obsess it. And don't you dare for a second believe that it is not beautiful.

Decades ago, black women weren't really afforded the opportunity to engage in conversations around beauty and skin care. Times have changed, and the conversations going around are a lot more diverse and inclusive, but the negative aspect of having so much information so readily available is that it can get slightly confusing about where to turn and who to listen to. Luckily enough for you, I have summarized a few of the most important elements that you should incorporate into your skincare routine to ensure that you maintain your natural outer glow.

Get vitamin D. As black people; we tend to need more vitamin D than our white counterparts. Due to the melanin in our bodies, it's harder for us to absorb vitamin D from the sun, so we have a higher chance of vitamin D insufficiency. It's educating ourselves to understand that being vitamin D deficient leads to host of so many health-related issues. So I'm here to tell you, sis, that you need to get a good quota of sunlight each day. To get your D-juice, go for a walk, sit or sunbathe if necessary. Do what you must to get the sun rays we need. If you don't have the privilege of a warm climate and you can't increase your Vitamin D intake by getting enough sunlight, eating more fatty fish and seafood, eating fortified foods such as cow or plant-based milk, fortified cereals, and orange juice, or getting Vitamin D supplements to ensure an adequate intake.

Adopt a good skincare routine that will help with acne spots, hyperpigmentation, and dark spots, which affect us more than other skin types. Our skin is definitely more susceptible to scarring, so we need to ensure we maintain a good skincare routine to help with our skin moisture and try consult a black dermatologist as they will understand our skin conditions much better.

However do your research before applying any product to your skin. Just because it comes in a fancy bottle or costs an arm and a leg doesn't necessarily mean that it will work for you. Our skin is different, and that means we all have different needs as well. Get to know your skin type. Research what ingredients are in certain products and whether they're compatible with your skin or not.

Our skin needs water to repair cells and skin elasticity. We've all heard the saying, *'black don't crack'*. So, let's keep up that ideology, ladies. The more hydrated we are, the better our skin health. We need to be drinking water. The skin is the largest organ in our bodies, and we need to nurture it. Water flushes out toxins and allows blood to flow. Drinking enough water improves skin tone, prevents premature aging, promotes faster healing, helps acne (for all those ladies suffering from skin problems), tightens skin, and promotes a healthy gut and clear skin. The list goes on. So we know what we need to do. Get those glasses ready, so we can create an army of water-loving black women

Your Hair

Your hair, my sister, is your crown. Each strand, each piece, and each follicle represents a unique part of you and your cultural heritage. It is a symbol of your unique beauty. It tells a story about who you truly are. Embrace and be proud of that.

The reason I say this is because I don't know about you, but I used to feel so ashamed about my hair. The fact that it was not straight, that it was wild, big, bold, and audacious.

It was always the first thing people noticed about me when I entered a room. In those moments, all I wanted to do would be to shrink and crawl into a hole so deep that no one would ever find me. Then the complete opposite happened I went through a period of severe breakage, thinning edges, and split ends, and simply the lack of education on how to revive and take care of it, left me feeling distressed. But looking at where I am today, I can definitely say that I have come a long way with my hair care journey and acceptance thereof.

All those things that they said about your hair, that it is unattractive or that you somehow need to change it, are not true. We, as black women, do love to change our hairstyles, embrace a new look, or simply wear it natural. Whether it be long or short, thick or thin, braids or twists, weaves or wigs, we have turned it around over the past few years, and we are all on the same journey of learning to love our natural hair unapologetically. So if you are on the same journey of learning to love your hair unapologetically, here are a few handy tips to keep in mind.

- **Wash** your hair at least once a week. This will help prevent an excessive build-up of dandruff and hair products which can be damaging to your hair.
- **Moisturize** your hair using the LOC method (in essence, you apply liquid, oil, and cream) or apply a store-bought daily moisturizer.

- Make sure that you use **natural ingredients** because certain harsh chemicals damage the follicles that aid in hair growth, making it even harder for our hair to grow. Shea butter and black soap are excellent for hair growth.
- Do **nightly scalp massages**. Massaging your scalp at night with a little bit of oil will help contribute to hair growth because massaging helps blood and the necessary nutrients to flow to the scalp and nourish it. Plus, imagine how relaxing it feels with a well-oiled scalp before bed. It is just sheer joy.
- Keep wearing those **protective hairstyles** when you need to. These include twists, braid outs, faux locs, braids, cornrows, crochet, head wraps, updos and weaves. Girl. Just keep an eye on those edges.
- **Love your natural hair too**. Embrace it as it is, and stop trying to change it. All types of diversity are beautiful: skin, body, culture, and hair included. Anyone who fails to see or understand that, are the ones who lose out on the greatest learning opportunities.

As we close off this chapter, I want to leave you with 7 daily tips on what you can do every day to love yourself and your body even better.

❇ **Commitment.** Honestly, I feel like the fact that you are here reading this means that you acknowledge that there are changes that you can make. So, I am proud of you for that. On those days when it's especially hard, remind yourself: I am a woman on a mission to build a healthier relationship with her body and her skin, with all of it. The more times you say it, the easier it will become for you to follow through on that promise to yourself.

❊ **Drop the narrative that changing certain things about yourself will magically make you happier because it will not**. You are valuable and precious, just as you are. Don't get me wrong a good makeover to enhance your outer look does wonders for our confidence and self esteem. When you're feeling good on the outside you automatically feel good on the inside. But it is mostly short lived as it can't mend the healthy choices we make, or mask your true feelings.

❊ **Get to know your body because to love it, you have to be familiar with the whole of it.** So, slow down and listen to all of the messages that it is communicating to you. You will honestly be shocked at how knowing all of you makes it so much easier to love yourself.

❊ **Do things that make you feel fabulous**. That can look like setting some time aside to rub your favorite lotion on your body. Maybe it's wearing your favorite pair of pants because they hug you in all of the right places and look especially flattering on you. These small acts of love are all about training your brain to associate certain actions with the feeling of L.O.V.E.

● **Sink deeply into that practice of body gratitude**. Every day wherever you are: driving to work, just getting out of bed, taking the kids to school, preparing your dinner, think of the characteristics that you love most about yourself. Is it your brilliant smile that lights up whatever room you enter? Your kind, compassionate and selfless heart? The shape of your eyes? Or lungs that carry you through your exercises?

● **Express yourself through your clothing**. Your body is the canvas, and the clothes you wear are the paint. So allow what you put on yourself to act as a form of creative expression. Be intentional in wearing clothes that make you feel sexy, powerful, and unstoppable.

● **Remember that your body is a living, breathing, and miraculous thing**. It's not inappropriate. Or too much. The shade of your skin or the size of your tummy does not and should not define how valuable you are.

Being loved by me is more than enough to create joy wherever I am and wherever I'm standing. So I will tell myself today and forever more…*I love you…I love you….I love you.* I hope that you do the same for yourself as well.

AFFIRMATIONS FOR LOVING OUR BODIES

My body deserves infinite love and care. Therefore, I will nourish and care for it as it should.

Each curve and contour on my body is a work of art and a blessed reminder that I am alive, well, healthy, and thriving.

I can be an example, a role model for other black women and young black girls on how they can love their bodies as is.

I am allowed to love myself.

I will embrace my body as it changes in all its seasons. It works tirelessly to keep me alive. The best that I can do is to sing infinite praise of its miraculous work.

My body is not an apology. I will not apologize for its presence. Its existence and its loudness.

I am beautiful and graceful. I will allow myself to be who I am. Not what others think I should be.

THREE
EMOTIONAL SELF-CARE

Sometimes peace won't always feel like bliss and tranquility, but a lot like chaos. Sitting with the messiest of emotions, acknowledging their existence, letting them shake and unsettle you, and then allowing them to move right through you. Then, once they've passed, allow yourself to gently move on with your day.

BEING a black woman sometimes means having to hold your anger out of fear of being dubbed the stereotypical "angry, bitter, and resentful" black woman. But in all honesty, we have so much to be angry about—being gaslit by our white superiors and the passive-aggressive jokes our white colleagues make about us. Not being afforded the same opportunities as our white counterparts. It bothers and pains me when someone from another race tells me to chill out, to stop being overly dramatic, or to tone down, or when they say, "you're so loud" or "too aggressive". Am I not allowed to express my emotions without being chastised? I don't want to be labeled as something that I am not.

I am a black woman, and I have emotions. So that means that some days are going to have highs, while others are going to be on the lower end. I get days where I feel deliriously excited and passionate about things and days where I feel indifferent. I have my strong days too. Days where I want to do nothing more than be independent, and the days where I just want to be held because I feel weak and I, too, need someone to hold onto. A shoulder to cry on. Or purely just my own space. So it's emotionally exhausting when I have to battle the negative stereotypes that are painted on me simply because I am a black woman. Why don't I deserve the opportunity to be vulnerable? To embrace the ups and downs of life like so many other women out there are allowed to?

WHY EMOTIONAL SELF-CARE MATTERS

Spending time with our emotions. Identifying, acknowledging them, and learning to uncover their meaning is what emotional self-care is all about. It's important because this is how we teach ourselves to overcome the traumas that we experience. It's how we learn to feel more confident about who we are and how we learn to overcome life's struggles and relationship challenges.

Our emotions relate directly to how we feel every day, and thus it impacts the decisions that we make on a daily basis and how we treat ourselves and those who are around us. A couple of years ago, just before work, I stepped into a coffee shop to grab some coffee. It was a bit of a crazy morning, so I didn't get the chance to make myself a cup at home like I usually would. There was this sweet lady in front of me. She ordered her coffee and she was reaching inside her handbag to grab her purse. The whole bag and its contents drop to the floor. She drops to the floor too, and in a coffee shop crowded and filled with people, she starts crying right then and there. I didn't understand at first. In my mind, I thought "Lady, just pick the stuff up. There's no need to make a scene about it," and seconds later, it dawned on me that she was having an emotional breakdown. I walked up to her, helped her gather the belongings from the floor, and asked her what was wrong. "It's all too much. I just want to let myself be sad. I want to let myself cry. Today is one of those days where I don't want to have it all together."

If you don't make space for your emotions, they're going to force their way into your life. They are sneaky like that and truly have a funny way of catching up to us. One moment you think you're fine, ordering your coffee and going about your day as you normally would, and then the next moment, you're having a complete meltdown in a coffee shop somewhere. So, this is why it is so crucial to allow yourself to feel what you need to feel without any judgment or harsh criticism.

If you choose to numb yourself to certain emotions like sadness, then you're essentially going to start numbing yourself to other emotions, too like happiness and excitement. The most amazing part about being human is that the whole experience is so diverse. And those experiences that we encounter when we're met with sadness are what make joy and happiness all the more incredibly delightful to experience.

Struggling with our emotions only causes us to struggle even more. I get it, sometimes you are under the impression that you just can't deal with your sadness or it feels like an inconvenience at that time, but let me ask you this, don't you think it's better to deal with it right then and there, rather than waiting on it to sneak up on you unexpectedly on a random day? Like my dear friend in that coffee shop? You wouldn't wait a month or week to treat a broken ankle or an arm. We should apply the same logic when we're dealing with our emotions.

Steps for taking care of our emotional health

In times of great distress, the best thing that we can do for each other is to listen to the message that the heart is sending out. There's so much there to uncover.

One of the greatest blessings of living in the era that we are in, is the open conversations around mental health. People aren't as afraid anymore to talk about their mental health struggles. When one person does so, it opens up the doorway for others to talk about their struggles as well. I love seeing black women go to therapy. I love seeing them take charge of their mental health and work towards healing because there really is a limit on how much we can hold and hoard until it suffocates us. Before I start sharing valuable tips and insights on what we can do to take better care of our emotional health, I want to share these nuggets of wisdom that I learned from a therapist.

"**Normal**" doesn't exist. So many of us are looking for some sort of reassurance or validation that we're doing things the right way. Whether or not we're normal. We look at our career or life expectations and ask, "*what will other people say about these?*" My question is, "*what do you have to say?*" Society has brainwashed us into thinking that our life will be over if we don't take a certain route, and I think that's completely nonsensical. If you want to be a homemaker, bake bread, and make all your sauces from scratch, it's okay. If you want to live child-free and be a digital nomad and spend your life traveling and working from anywhere around the world, that's perfectly okay too. Your life is yours! You set the terms and conditions. If it makes you feel content, at peace, and incredibly alive, then it shouldn't matter what anyone else thinks or says.

Things you own or what you've achieved don't define your worth. I love to see my fellow black sisters doing well with themselves, but it bothers me when people use possessions as a measure of success. It's all about the car you drive, the house you live in, and the shoes you wear. Pushing this mentality is, more often than not, what makes people feel ashamed about themselves or makes them feel like they are behind in life. It makes us overlook the progress that we are making and the blessing right before our eyes. Success is a state of mind, and I say, "*As long as you're not where you used to be yesterday, a week, or a month ago, you are winning and definitely killing it.*"

When people critique or criticize you, it's not really about you. It's about them and the insecurities that they're projecting on you. So next time someone comes raining on your parade, try not to take it too seriously—there's something in their lives that they're just unhappy about.

Regardless of where you want to be, remember to be present in the now. Life is happening right now, so embrace it with all of your senses.

You are the one who has to hold yourself accountable. There are certain battles in life that you (and only you) will be responsible for fighting. When you step up and take full responsibility for your choices and your actions, anything that you set your mind to will hardly seem impossible.

You don't have to beat yourself up for things you're still trying to figure out. The best piece of advice—more like words of wisdom—is that no one really has it all figured out. We're all just as confused as the next person, so we should give ourselves some grace and compassion as we work on navigating this messy world.

It's okay to cut toxic people out of your life. (I've got a whole discussion planned for you on this topic, so I won't go into too much detail at this stage). If someone (a family member or a friend) makes you feel insignificant or bad about yourself, they do not deserve a place in your life. It's okay and incredibly healthy to set strict boundaries with them and say no to their negative energy.

If you're happy, be happy. Feel your joy fully without restraint, and don't worry too much about what will and will not happen. We sometimes rob ourselves of that divine opportunity to experience joy as it comes because we're conditioned to always expect the worst. Stop letting things that you cannot control, prevent you from living your best life.

What to say to help set healthy boundaries with family, friends, and work colleagues

Sis, we have to learn to put ourselves first. I've mentioned this before, but I think I have to mention again that we need to enforce and maintain healthy boundaries. Weak boundaries, like not speaking up for yourself, invite a lot of disrespect and unhealthy access to your emotions, energy, and time. Healthy boundaries are what make healthy relationships, but so many of us are afraid to walk that route because we are under the impression that people will hate us or that we are going to be labeled as selfish or unaccommodating. The truth is that if someone is not willing to respect the boundaries that you are enforcing, they don't really deserve to be in your life. Period. Boundaries are one way of saying "I love you" to ourselves and to others because we cannot love well when we're overwhelmed or feeling burdened.

As someone who has struggled with being "*the good girl*", I didn't always have the language to express the healthy boundaries that I needed to enforce. I agreed to do things that I didn't necessarily feel like doing. I abandoned and neglected myself because other people always had to come first, in my opinion. But the same as with anything worthwhile, it takes time to get into the habit of expressing yourself and setting healthy boundaries. We are taught that we should be "*agreeable*" and "*selfless*", and not being available makes us difficult. Reclaiming that silenced voice of mine has by far been the best thing that I could have done for myself. I learned to cultivate a deeper relationship with myself and developed a more trusting relationship with my intuition. When setting boundaries, we allow ourselves to pour into our relationships, our work, and everything else that is in between; from a cup that is full instead of one that is tethering on empty.

Some ways through which you can enforce healthy boundaries include doing the following:

- Understanding what you are and aren't available for
- Asking for help when you need it
- Communicating and speaking out about how you feel
- Saying no, and not feeling a need to feel guilty about doing so
- Growing the language or vocabulary that doesn't necessarily come easy to you.

Here are a few additional statements you can use as a template to help create and enforce healthier boundaries.

❈ **With your time commitments:** I'm not available at that specific time. Let's find a time that's more suitable for both of us. Would "x" work for you?

❈ **With Gossip:** I don't feel comfortable talking about someone when they're not in my presence because I know how I would feel if someone did that to me. I'd rather talk about something else. I don't want to be a part of a conversation that won't leave me feeling good.

❀ **When you need your space and some alone time**: The best thing that I need to do for myself right now is to honor my needs. I just need to spend some time alone to fill my cup so that I can show up for you as the best version of me possible.

❀ **Unsolicited comments**: I don't appreciate those comments that you make about "x". I would really appreciate it if you kept them to yourself.

❀ **Work hours:** My hours are "x" and I do not work on weekends because it interferes with my family time. I'll be happy to look at that for you during my working hours.

❀ **Socializing:** Thanks for the invite. I would like to be at home by "x" and it doesn't sound like something that I'd enjoy, but have fun!

❀ **Aggressive communication:** I don't appreciate that particular tone that you're using with me. This conversation is something that I'm willing to continue only if you're willing to calm down a bit.

It's not going to be the smoothest process, but I can tell you that it will be so worth it in the end.

Make gratitude a part of your life. Shifting the focus from *'everything good'* that is going on for you, instead of focusing on *'everything not so good'* going on is a great way to change your entire outlook on life.

Furthermore, making a conscious choice to focus on gratitude will put you in a better mood and help you decrease your stress levels.

Here are some tips to make gratitude a part of your life and your family's too:

- **Choose a specific time of the day** (breakfast or dinner) and take turns talking about something great that happened to each of you throughout the day.
- **Model gratitude in front of your children**. Thank people for helping you, and make sure that you comment on things that you appreciate about them.
- **Instead of showering the kids with gifts**, save the gift-giving for special occasions or look for ways through which the kids can earn the things that they want as a way of making those things more meaningful when they come. That way, they will be less likely to take those things for granted.
- **Tell someone that you love them**, or acknowledge that trait or thing that you appreciate about them most. Y'all, life is short and as heavy as it is to think about, we never know when our last interactions will be with our loved ones, so don't let that opportunity to

shower them with kind, loving words slip right past you.
- **Keep images and quotes around your house that remind you to be grateful.** Ever get those days where you feel as if your whole life is falling apart, but you read something and are instantly reminded that all will be okay? That is the power of words. Allow them to be the light in your life when you can't seem to find any.
- **Say thank you to someone.** There are millions of people around us, and therefore that means there isn't a shortage of people who we can say thank you to. The shop assistant who helped you pack your grocery bags. The gentleman who held the door open for you. The barista who made your coffee. Leave a kind message at a coworker's desk. You can be as creative as you want with your thank you's—the sky's the limit!

Journaling is vital to emotional healing

Journaling. Writing is so therapeutic. The process of transferring what was in my head onto paper (so that I can review them at a later stage) has helped me reduce so much of the anxiety that I have. Some people think that they have to be the greatest writers on the planet for them to consider journaling, or they have to have all the stationary that are Pinterest and Instagram worthy. That couldn't be further from the truth. Journaling is about you.

It's about building a connection with yourself, so you have to let go of the expectation of your journal looking a certain way. Write whatever comes up. The more attention you place on the feelings that feel right, the easier the practice will be for you.

Here are a few additional tips to help you create a habit out of your journaling practice.

❊ **Consistency matters**. It's something that you have to do regularly. It shouldn't be that thing that you do every four months or so. The more you do it, the more flow you'll find in the process because you'll have a clear idea of what works and doesn't work for you. Remember. It's not about writing pages upon pages. If all you can manage is half a page or a couple of sentences daily, that's good enough.

❊ **Time of day**. Play around with the times that you find most suitable for you. If you're a morning person, squeeze in some time in the mornings for a quick writing session. If you prefer the evenings, then schedule some time for yourself after you've left work. It's really helpful to have a consistent time because that's something that will keep you committed to the process. Also, it's great to have a daily journaling goal, but if that doesn't work for you, a couple of days a week works just as well, too.

❋ **Write from a place of honesty.** You are writing to you. Not for anybody else, so don't be afraid to be vulnerable and candid with what you share in your journal. You don't have to worry about what it will look like to the world out there. Your journal is your place of peace. Allow yourself to be free.

❋ **Make it a special time for you.** You want it to be an overall enjoyable experience, not just another thing that you "have" to do. You can create this element of luxury by using a favorite pen of yours or even making yourself a cup of hot cocoa every time you get cozied up to write. You can even create a special playlist for yourself to create that ambiance that you want.

❋ **Use prompts if you're afraid you might get writer's block.** For me, I make a list of the little things that make me happy. With these, you can expand a little bit more on why these things are significant to you and your joy. You can also have emotional check-ins with yourself. Like how you're feeling or how your mood fluctuates throughout the day. *What things should or could you let go of? Are there any victories that are worthy of being celebrated?*

Setting Time for Mindfulness Activities

Engage in mindfulness activities. It's so easy to be pulled in a multitude of directions in this noisy world. That is what leaves our thoughts and emotions highly strung and scattered all over the place. We can even take a moment or two to breathe, recenter our thoughts, and enjoy the beauty of being able to be present in our bodies. So if you're one, who's always pressed for time and barely has a moment to focus on yourself, here are four mindfulness exercises for you to try.

❃ **Be mindful in your interactions**. The way you interact with your people matters. It's about being as non-judgemental as possible in your relationships and remaining engaged and present in the conversation or interaction that you are having. So instead of scrolling through your phone throughout the whole conversation, give them your undivided attention and listen to understand what they are saying, not simply respond. Be present in the moment. So many of us are using our phones and replacing them for those personal interactions, but it can't respond back the way we want it to. So we need to revert back to more personal interactions which leaves a more positive emotional state of mind.

❃ **Be the kind of friend that you would want to have**. Show up for your friends and your loved ones by recognizing and learning how they might want you to show up for them in the various stages and transitions of their lives.

Is it through affirming text messages? Coffee chats? Acts of service? I think here you need to foster healthy relationships by making time for yourself and family and friends around you. So you need to strike that right balance between time for yourself, which is very important, and time with friends, and that equal combination is the key to healthy emotional wellbeing.

❋ **Share and ask for help**. I think we sometimes get ashamed of the struggles that we are facing, so we shrink into our own little worlds and try to fight these battles all on our own. Sharing, and being our most vulnerable with our friends, creates a strong bond that is nearly impossible to swerve.

❋ **Be creative with how you spend time with each other**. Remember, the way we spend time with our friends doesn't have to be too time-consuming, nor does it have to involve anything too fancy. You can spend some quality time by exercising in the mornings or scheduling a facetime chat during your lunch break. If you're lucky enough to live close enough to your friends, you can meet up before work for a quick coffee date. If you have errands to run, do them together. There's nothing quite like those chats and laughs with your friend in the produce aisle. Just saying.

Friendship—well, relationships in general—are a lot like flowers. They do not thrive, survive, and bloom all on their own. They need sunlight, water, and tenderness. Giving them those things that they need, will ensure that you never feel alone.

Cutting off the toxic people from your life

These are the types of people who you should distance yourself from:

The ones who take. They will take and take from you and the friendship/relationship without bringing anything else to the table. Friendship is a two-way street. So if you think that you are the only one committing and bringing something to the table, you might need to reevaluate the situation.

The unsupportive ones. Good friends or partners are the ones who support you in all that you do, even if they don't necessarily understand why you are doing the things that you're doing.

The manipulators. These people only think about one person, and it's them. They will do anything to get their way, even if it puts you and your interests in jeopardy.

The chronic complainers. Negativity is contagious, so if you spend too much time around negative people, you'll find yourself developing the same character traits as them.

The ones who criticize you without end, the jealous types, the ones with the victim mindset, and the ones who just can't seem to stop disappointing you.

You need to protect your energy as much as you can. It's not always easy, especially when those people are our family because we are taught that family sticks it out together through thick and thin. Isn't it? But seeing and recognizing those unhealthy patterns for what they are, and deciding that you want no part of it in this life that you are building, is a powerful and incredibly brave decision to make.

AFFIRMATIONS TO HELP YOU REMEMBER THAT JOY IS YOUR BIRTHRIGHT

I deserve an absolute and endless amount of bliss to flow through my life.

I will fight daily to cling to the joy that I am creating. No one, or anything, gets to take that away from me.

When I focus on joy, it flows more effortlessly into my life.

I will stand daily in the joy that I am planting from within.

The overflow of good that I have in my life comes from having a vision that is focused on prosperity and happiness.

Life may not always be good, but regardless I choose to hold onto the belief that there's a better life ahead because I am the one who gets to create and write their own story.

I will not allow anybody else's mood or negative energy to dim my own light.

I am present in my life.

My days flow effortlessly with radiance.

I serve with compassion and speak with kindness.

I see the goodness in others, and that is why joy will never stop chasing and finding me—wherever I am in this life.

FOUR
MENTAL SELF-CARE—HEALING THE HEART AND MIND

To live. To see things through. To get to that point where we are doing more than just surviving…

I KNEW I was healing and coming back home to myself when I rediscovered some of my old passions. I knew I was healing when I started listening more to myself than to other people. I knew I was healing when I wasn't as afraid to dig deep and reflect on my identity. I knew I was healing when I bravely shed through the layers of skin that no longer fit me, when I accepted responsibility instead of deflecting from it.

I knew I was healing when I started honoring and accepting all of those ways in which I had changed. We all stray every now and again from ourselves, but eventually, we make it back home.'

I have to keep it real and speak my truth here, like I said this is the platform where we can be open and share our secrets. Healing ain't easy, I've found it so damn hard y'all. I won't lie to you. It is a process that is as scary as it is messy. I think that's one of the reasons why so many of us choose to avoid it like you would a dingy alleyway at midnight. Most of us black women suppress our emotions and leave our superwoman shields on to prevent ourselves from having to talk about our emotions. We drown ourselves in work *"just to keep busy"*, so that we don't have to think about what's really bothering us. It's the pain that comes from having to dig up fears, memories, and feelings that we would rather much forget that makes us choose to limp our way through life rather than pursue that bright path to freedom.

One of the things that kept me really stuck throughout my healing journey was that resistance. I didn't want to visit those painful moments I had experienced and look deeper into the wounds they had left. I spent so much time trying to validate the existence of those wounds and keep them open so that they would remain relevant—a justifiable excuse for my anger—I didn't want to take an alternative and harder route and redefine my own identity.

I wanted to walk the path all on my own because I was afraid I would be judged or that no one else would understand. There was also a version of me that I wanted people to see, "*the unbothered black woman,*" the "*I'm a strong black woman. I can handle this and move on*". '*I don't need any man,*' but that left me feeling more alone than you could ever imagine. I looked around me, and all I could see were women who seemed to be crushing it in their professional and personal lives, but what about me? Why couldn't I seem to get it right? It wasn't until one day a friend saw behind my facade and asked me what was up. I broke down and told her all that I was experiencing. About how overwhelmed I'd been by the grief over a lost relationship. And you know what she did? She listened. She held me, and that made me feel as if I had just released a ton off my shoulders. Navigating a room that you've never been in is a lot scarier when you're trapped in the dark. The light is what makes it feel easier and safer to navigate. I think that's how we should approach and handle our journey to healing. We should find that one who is light, the one who will make the journey a little less lonely.

We're too focused on perfectionism because life has taught us that there is no room at all for mistakes. We want to get this process right down to a T. That's why we spend hours and money on "self-help" books that will help us get over it in some ten-step regimen. But let me tell you, there is no such thing as the perfect life, home, marriage, children, or body, whatever social media or YouTube bloggers lead us to believe. They are big distortions of the truth. It's not real life; it's entertainment, it's a job, and we can't let it impact our state of mind. We all strive for different things, so don't compare yourself to anyone hoping to have the same unrealistic standards. I believe that when we allow ourselves to crawl, to ease into the process, and take it as slow as we need, we awaken to the understanding that we are not the only ones struggling with this perfectionism thing and giving ourselves the grace to take things one step at a time is how we see the greatest amount of progress. It's what allows us to recognize that somewhere inside of us, our wounded inner person is looking at us through tear-filled eyes, marveling at how far we have come and are going to get.

Sometimes we can always make excuses waiting for the right time to get started on the journey. There are so many things that we're waiting to happen or not happen. We're going to get started when we have more time on our hands. When we're not too consumed by our work commitments. When we're "*ready*." Does this sound a little like something that you can relate to? Here's a little reality check... You will never be ready, so the best place to start is where you are right now. I promise you; you'll figure things out as you go along your way.

When it comes to healing, we have to acknowledge that there are certain things that we have to leave behind—our identity, who we thought we were, certain beliefs, and sometimes, even people too. So sit with that pain for as long as you need to. That can only be an indication that you are making space for something new.

UNPACKING CHILDHOOD TRAUMA

Girl, I'm going to be honest with you. When we start our journey, we have to start from scratch, and that starts with our childhood. Our childhood affects us more than we think. To heal, we sometimes have to unpack the past, which in turn gives light to the future. We grow up as adults, not realizing that the impacts of our childhood seep into our very souls and unconscious minds. Without peeling back the fabrics of what we experienced as children, it can sometimes hinder our healing process, and we can never get to the root cause of why we behave a certain way today. *So, what does it mean and look like to have unresolved childhood trauma in your life?*

- Running from your emotions and trying to find solace with alcohol, drugs, and other substances
- It shows up as codependency in your relationships.

- It shows low self-esteem and not being able to see your worth.
- It's living in survival mode.
- It shows up as needing a caretaker in your relationship, and not a partner.
- It's hyper-independence.
- Becoming a workaholic
- Not being able to relax or enjoy your downtime.
- It's a lack of clarity when it comes to your own needs or not knowing how to fulfill them yourself.
- It's a lack of clear communication with others.

What our childhood traumas do is distort the perception that we have of ourselves. So many of you are magnetic black women with the most infectious personality. And you light up every room you enter, but the problem is, you struggle to see that. If you could see yourself through the way that everybody else sees you, you would recognize how special, loved, and unique you are.

I also want to highlight that childhood trauma is a lot of things. It's not just violence or sexual abuse. There are so many things in our childhoods that we grow up thinking are normal when the actual truth is that they are not. As a black community, we need to take ownership of generational trauma. We have layers and layers of unaddressed cultural trauma dating back to our turbulent history that simply manifests into years of inherited painful childhood experiences. Whether positive or negative, they all impact how we behave as adults. To heal, you can only address the cultural issues. Childhood trauma also looks like having been denied your reality by your parents. It's having been told that your emotions aren't relevant or that you were not allowed to experience certain emotions. Or maybe you had a parent who was hyper-focused on appearance, so you grew to be uncomfortable in your skin or your body. It's having a parent who could not regulate their emotions. Remember, just because certain things may be common does not mean they are normal. As we begin shifting the norm, we cannot allow society to determine what is normal or not.

Tips For Healing Childhood Trauma

The process of healing your childhood trauma will require a lot of work in the beginning. It will be incredibly uncomfortable at times too, but it'll certainly be a very rewarding journey.

But how do we put in the work and heal those traumas exactly?

Just like we do when we are wounded on our body, we locate the wound: we look for the source of pain. You could spend time looking into your family history. This would give you a great opportunity to understand your past. Who were your great great grandparents? Learning who your great ancestors were can give you a clear picture of who you are and where you came from, it can give you a sense of self-worth, and boost your sense of belonging and identity. By doing this exercise it can sometimes fill in those gaps that you question about yourself.

Look around your daily life to find your potential triggers. What things in your daily life heighten your anxiety, make you sad, or more anxious than you should feel? It can also be particularly helpful to ask yourself whether or not it is helpful, to focus so much of your attention on these things daily. Being of black heritage, we know our ancestors lived through turbulent times. They faced persecution and inequality and lived through the peak of racial discrimination, we only experience a portion of that today. So it should give you the courage to keep fighting. If they could live through difficult times and find the courage to keep going, you need to be able to do the same in the 20th century.

Start paying attention to how you soothe yourself. Are you trying to numb away your emotions by scrolling mindlessly on social media? Do you turn to food and comfort eat your way? Do you prefer keeping yourself endlessly busy so that you don't have time to sit and think about what it is that's bothering you?

Start connecting the dots with memories from your childhood. What kind of parent(s) did you have? Did you have one who scrutinized everything that you did? Or the parent who tried to control you? Or were they more the fixer-type parent who did nothing but drive you to anxiety? Or did you have to grow up quickly and be a mother to younger siblings? Was your father around? Did that affect you? Did you see too much as a child? Did you like your skin color as a child? Did your parents help you combat that? Did you deal with racism as a child? These questions will help you pull apart your childhood and dissect it, so you can start healing from them.

Take that inner child as your adult self. This process or step is about being the person that your inner child needed at that time. It's re-parenting and re-mothering yourself. What would the nurturer, the logical, authentic adult self, say to that wounded inner child? Think about all the things you would have wanted to hear as a child growing up, and shower yourself with those loving words.

You were not loved in a way that you wanted or deserved to be loved. You were raised by unconscious parents who had unresolved traumas in their own lives, and as a result, it negatively came out in their parenting style. Here is an example of something that would be helpful to say to yourself in those moments when you feel completely helpless:

'You are worthy of love. That's the one thing that I want to say to you right now. All of the negatives, the beliefs and the toxic conditioning are something that you will conquer so that you do not project the same kind of wounds on to your children.'

Share. The more we talk about the challenging things we've been through, the easier it becomes for us to deal with and navigate the struggles they sometimes come with. And by sharing, I don't necessarily mean talking to other people about the struggles. That is also a productive tactic, but I know that not everybody will be comfortable doing that. You can write about the experiences. Describe how those experiences wounded you, how you reacted, and what that experience has taught you. Sharing is such an important aspect in healing because that is how we let it all out and learn to let go.

CHOOSING TO HEAL-THIS IS WHY WE DO IT

Healing is how we let go of feeling powerless over our lives. It's saying yes to growth and no to being stuck in the same place in your life for all eternity. It's how you say yes to life and get life to say yes to you. It's as simple as that. We choose to heal because we deserve to give ourselves that spectacular shot at life.

Here are 2 reasons for you to choose emotional healing.

1. We do it to break generational curses. We need to consciously think about how we are impacted by our pasts and how those elements influence our futures. If we do not dress the wounds where we've been hurt, we're going to start bleeding on the innocent bystanders around us. My children, nor yours, deserve to suffer because I was too afraid to deal with the past events that tried to traumatize me. They deserve to be raised by an emotionally healthy parent and thus will teach them to be emotionally healthy adults as well.

2. You'll regain your spark and start to enjoy life once again. So many of us are held back because we are holding on too tightly to the past. The effect that has on us, is it slows us down. If you took a hiking backpack and filled it with rocks, you'd have a pretty hard time making your way up to the top of the mountains, but if you stopped and gently started reducing the weight of the bag by leaving those rocks behind, the journey to the top won't seem like such a burden. Healing gives you the freedom to create a life for yourself outside of that trauma or that heartbreak you experience. It permits you to be in the driver's seat. So take yourself where you need to go, fill in the gaps that need to be filled, and enhance your existence. You do not have to keep yourself imprisoned in the past.

Coping Mechanisms for Healing

Sis, before we jump right into a couple of healthier coping mechanisms, I want to share with you a couple of things that you should remember about the healing journey and all it entails.

It's something that gets easier when we're able to figure out what's actually going on. Don't run away from it. Run toward it. Acknowledge that it's there, and once you do, you'll be able to figure out what steps it is that you need to take.

* **Discomfort doesn't make you a bad person**, nor does it mean that you're doing anything wrong. You can let yourself soften, be vulnerable, and open up with the pain you feel. Don't try to mask them by continuing as you've been doing. Being vulnerable doesn't mean being a 'weak black woman.' It means the opposite: being strong enough to be open and honest about it. It's good and will help you go far in your healing journey.

* **It's important to chase after those things that make your spirit feel at ease**. When you engage in activities that you enjoy, you're creating some sort of buffer between you and that discomfort that exists. There is still plenty of room available for life to happen as you heal. It doesn't necessarily all have to come to a standstill.

* **Forgiveness is a vital element of the process**. Remember, forgiveness is not about them; it's about you and what it can do for you. Through my own healing experiences, I have realized that it is far better to choose forgiveness than give in to bitterness. It wasn't something that I always wanted to do, but soon after I did, I would feel a lightness that I couldn't describe come up in my heart. It felt like a veil being lifted from my eyes, and I could finally see clearly again. It changed my entire experience of how I related to the past.

* **Love wins.** This sounds like a cliche or another line from a cheesy self-help book, but it does. I healed because I wanted to be loved. To radiate and give a healthy kind of

love to those people who deserve it. Love is what heals our shattered hearts, so as long as we've got love as our guiding light, we can be rest assured that we're going to be okay.

Positive self-talk in our day-to-day lives

The effects of systematic racism on black women's emotional and mental health are unavoidable. Think about it from this perspective. When black women lose a loved one due to something as traumatic as police violence, they have to go through the whole process of grief and try to understand why that particular thing happened. It's also about the emotional energy that is needed to fight that injustice. The stress of having to deal with that pressure is one of the things that make black women so particularly vulnerable to depression.

We also have to understand that due to the stigmas and a lack of trust in the healthcare system, black women are less likely to reach out and seek professional help for their mental health challenges. But what happens when mental health challenges aren't addressed? They worsen and rob us of that opportunity of a life well-lived.

Positive self-talk is one of the many ways that we can combat the negative effects that stress has on our emotional and mental wellbeing. It's not a cure-all and won't magically make all the evil of this world disappear, but it certainly is a good place to start to help you shift your mindset and focus on all the potential good that exists. When we engage in positive self-talk with ourselves, we are reinforcing the positive things that we believe and reduce the negatives.

The key to leveraging and getting the best out of your positive self-talk practice lies in understanding that the practice is rooted in curiosity—curiosity is what paves the way for lasting and sustainable healing. Your fears, your anxieties, and your pain have reasonable explanations. The key to understanding them lies in being unafraid and willing to explore what they mean.

Let's take a look at **an example of what positive self-talk may look like** in a normal day-to-day scenario.

So some things changed in your life, and it seems as though things no longer align with the goals that you have for yourself. This is hard for you because it seems you can no longer find the time and energy to do the things you enjoyed. You might even be slacking a little when it comes to your overall wellness and life goals.

The typical conversation that you'd have with yourself would go a little bit like this: *"Why am I such a mess? I am supposed to have my life together. I'm such a failure, and that is why I don't deserve any good things for myself."*

Trying the radical and gentle approach that encourages positive self-talk and leaning more towards compassion, may go on to sound a lot like this:

Why am I struggling so much? There is a need that is not being met, and the best thing to do for myself is to sit and try to understand what it is and where it comes from. What is it that I can change to get access to the care and love that I need in this current season of life? Stop here and do this exercise for a couple minutes.

Do you see how much of a difference it makes? A gentler approach is the most productive strategy that we can take when we are struggling.

When you're engaging in the practice of positive self-talk, you want to make sure that you are not lying to yourself. The conversation should be as authentic as possible.

Here are four practical tips that I want you to keep in mind.

1. Change your behavior. It's one thing to tell yourself that you are going to change your behaviors, and start thinking more positively in general and a completely different thing to actually make those changes that you're talking about making. If you continue to do things the way you're used to, and don't make the steps to change it up, it's going to be a lot more challenging than you think to integrate those positive changes into your life.

2. Make sure that you believe in what you're actually saying to yourself. I guess when you're in the middle of an emotional storm, kind, encouraging words can straight up feel forced, fake, and inauthentic. For example, if you've just experienced a devastating loss, saying something like "I am happy" will not feel true or resonate with you in that moment. Something like "I am not okay right now, but I am clinging on to the possibility that there is light at the end of the tunnel". Play around until you find the affirmation that rings true and resonates with you at that moment.

3. Enlist the help of a professional. Hyping yourself up is rarely ever the easiest thing to do, especially when there are other things, such as systematic racism, that one has to factor in. A black trained professional will help you see the bigger picture and help point out things that you yourself may be missing.

4. Challenge and question those negative thoughts and limiting beliefs that arise. You do not have to believe everything that your brain tells you about you. Ask yourself frequently and regularly, if what your brain is saying, is it accurate and balanced? And most importantly: where does that particular thought come from? Question every thought and dissect it to try and formulate its validity, don't let in sink in and absorb the belief that they are true. Negative thoughts have a way of lingering around and co-existing along side us day to day but challenge every one of them. Say this with me 'I am good enough just as I am' believe it, let it sit there. Next time you feel yourself heading to that negative place in your head switch it up with positive talk. I've jotted some positive affirmations you can start with in those times of need.

POSITIVE AFFIRMATIONS TO HELP YOU WITH YOUR HEALING

The healing journey is something personal and different to each and every one of us. I have found that one of the easiest ways in which we can help ourselves navigate the journey without comparing ourselves to someone else is by using words that are affirming. Love language affirmation is one of the top love languages for black women, so we need to make sure we make time for affirmations as it helps us stay focused amongst all the negativity and challenges that we face on a daily basis. "**Out loud**" is my preference and something that works. So I hope that these affirmations that I've written for you here resonate with you deeply and encourage you to keep working on you and for you because you are simply magic. Take them and say a few each day out aloud to yourself, in a mirror, in your car, on the school run, at your desk at work, before bed affirm your identity and own it.

I own my journey and this healing process that I am on. I am going to treat myself with nothing but empathy and compassion. My journey is mine and no one else's, so I will not dare compare it to someone else.

I look forward to a rich and fulfilling life, so I will acknowledge my inner child. I will listen to her and appreciate her for all of her values.

I am not hard to love. Even though I am still on my healing journey, I am perfectly worthy of love right now, just as I am.

I am heard. I am seen. I am loved; all of the parts of me are acknowledged, accepted, and appreciated.

I will be gentle and patient with myself. I know that this journey is going to be far from easy, but I am grateful for each day that comes my way and the strength that I am given to work through the pain.

I am choosing to set myself free by choosing to forgive.

I acknowledge all of my unresolved feelings with patience, self-acceptance, and grace.

I am unbelievable and unstoppable, and that is why I have made it as far as I have. I am resilient and spiritually strong, so I will keep going.

I am writing the story that I want to live.

Love is the one element that will help us weather the toughest of storms, but even in those times when it is hardest to find, I will still search relentlessly for its healing light.

I am giving full permission for peace to take over and lighten my spirit. With time, I can only hope that things will work out exactly as they are meant to.

I am so excited and looking forward to meeting the parts of me that I have always pushed toward the dark.

I am expanding far beyond the confines of how and what I was forced to think I am supposed to be. I am allowing myself to grow with and look forward to the possibilities that lie ahead.

I am a remarkable black woman, and I believe in myself, my capabilities, and my endless potential. I am choosing to protect and preserve my light by only focusing on the things that are feeding my growth.

I choose to root everything that I do in love because, with love as my compass, I know that my body, spirit, and I will find their way to perfect health again.

HELP OTHER BLACK WOMEN EMBARK ON THE ROAD TO RADICAL SELF-CARE

"Many of us have a hard time putting ourselves on our own priority list, let alone at the top of it. And that's what happens when it comes to our health as women. We are so busy giving and doing for others that we almost feel guilty to take that time out for ourselves."

MICHELLE OBAMA

Right at the start of the book, I mentioned that as black women, we are taught to sacrifice and put others first—our children, partners, and families. Because of our place in the racial and gender hierarchy, we are seen as constant labourers for our children, partners, families, and even in the workplace.

Without a doubt, this sense of sharing and caring for our community is a beautiful thing, but the source of authentic love for others lies in self-kindness, self-compassion, and self-care.

Just think back to a time in which you felt burnt out, over-stressed, and stretched in too many directions. When someone asked you to take part in a community fundraiser or a celebratory family gathering, perhaps you wanted to attend but said no. There was just nothing left to give.

That's the thing about self-neglect. It ends up impacting the very people you want so badly to help and protect.

When you are well-rested, you feed your body and mind the fuel it needs to function at their best, and you take time to do the things that give you a sense of purpose, everyone benefits. You are more likely to be fully present when someone needs you, and you become more capable of handling stress and challenging situations.

By this stage in the book, I would hope you have come to realize why you should prioritize yourself, empower your body, take care of your emotional health, and heal your heart and mind against past traumas.

Take a good look around you, though. How many black women in your life have done all this? Many of us are so consumed about fulfilling others' needs that we are still so reluctant to take proactive steps such as setting clear and healthy boundaries with friends, family, and work colleagues.

Thankfully, many black women are taking the podium now and espousing the importance of looking after yourself. Michelle Obama has often spoken about the necessity of holding fast to your own beliefs and values. "The only expectations I need to live up to are my own," she said.

Other renowned black activist speakers such as Stacey Abrams and Angela Davis have also stressed the importance of self-care, setting boundaries and prioritizing your needs amongst all the challenges.

You may not have the same platform or media access as these women, but you do have your own voice, and being part of a collective gives us a chance to share the power of self-healing, care, and love with other black women.

By leaving a review of this book on Amazon, you'll help other women squash the myth that the only needs that matter are everyone else's or the notion that we are infatigable, but by learning the core principles and practical tips for self-care; it is the key to empowerment as a black community.

Telling others what you have learnt from this book. Plus what to expect inside, will help our black sisters understand that radical self-care is the first step to being good to yourself, as a parent, friend, worker, and community member.

By spreading the word, you can be part of our radical self-care movement #theblackwomenselfcarerevolution.

Scan the QR code to leave a review or visit the link below!

https://geni.us/selfcare_review

FIVE
SPIRITUAL SELF-CARE

Spirituality is a journey we undertake to reclaim our individuality and hopefully, how we rediscover our ability to shine.

I HAVE BEEN THINKING a lot about spirituality lately, what it is, and what it particularly means to me.

Thinking about it made me realize what a particularly difficult topic and concept it is to define because it is not the same for all of us; therefore, its meaning resonates differently.

So I went out to ask some of my closest black sisters what spirituality means to them, and these are just a few of the answers that I got:

- It's a matter of being one with my mind, my body, and my spirit. It lies in knowing that I am a part of something that is far bigger than myself.
- It's being aware of who I truly am and finding rest, ease, and comfort in that knowledge.
- It's allowing myself to enjoy the gift of now by taking moments as they come and allowing myself the gift of the present moment.
- Unlearning anything about myself and having faith that my beliefs will carry me through. It's all about loving myself fully, as I am not feeling compelled to change anything about myself.
- It's being in touch with myself and saving that ability to look inwards when making decisions or through my interactions with others.
- It's honoring my soul and the souls of others. Choosing to see beyond the exterior and recognizing that within each of us lies an invaluable kind of beauty.

Black ancestors' spiritual healing is a practice that helps make sense of the world around us. It makes us realize who we truly are. We are not the body we seem to be, nor are we the mind or the ego telling us: "It's all about me." Sometimes things happen to or around us that we can't understand or derive meaning from. So when that happens, our spirituality steps in and helps us fill in the empty spaces. As black women, spirituality is how we maintain peace when the rest of the world is at war with us. The remarkable thing about this whole concept is that our guidance comes from just about anywhere: the inspiring stories about our black heroes, black art, the books that we read, and sermons we listen to—literally anywhere—but besides that, there are multiple other reasons why it's such a central theme in the life of an African woman. Let's check out some of those reasons.

It gives hope when it seems like there isn't any going around. Acknowledging our faith, and holding on to the belief that out there exists something that is far bigger than ourselves, is what gives us the confidence that we need to handle the curveballs that life throws at us with tenacity. When we are able to look within and find that place that reminds us that uncertainty is part of the human experience, it lessens the blow or the emotional impact all because we know that others have been where we are and they made it out just fine.

It gives a whole new meaning to this thing we call life. In a world that seemingly looks and feels as if evil is taking over, spirituality is what allows us to believe in the beauty of something good. It's what encourages us to be better people.

It adds more joy and contentment to our lives. Oh, nothing beats that feeling of knowing that everything is going to work out perfectly in your favor. I love resting in the knowledge that even though it may not seem so right now, everything is going to work out perfectly in my favor. Spirituality inclines us to keep an optimistic mindset (which shouldn't be confused with toxic positivity). This approach to life lessens the burden of having it all figured out on your own. When that happens, joy finds you and takes a seat at your table.

DECONSTRUCTING THE MYTHS ABOUT SPIRITUAL SELF-CARE

We are all seekers of truth, and one of the quickest ways to make it to that truth is through a spiritual journey or having something that you believe in. But a harsh reality to accept is that if you are on a spiritual journey, it can be so easy for people to mislead you or for you to even mislead yourself. I've had my fair share of ups and downs on my journey, but you know what? I wouldn't trade those experiences with anyone or anything because if not for those experiences, I wouldn't be here writing this book and enriching your life with the wisdom that I wish someone would have shared with me.

Myth 1: With spirituality, my life will go as planned. Spirituality makes us more patient and more accepting of the natural flow of our lives, but it doesn't make those ups and downs that we experience as we navigate life any less painful. So I want you to understand that spiritual wellness is not a "quick-fix" solution that will make all of your problems disappear; rather it equips you with the mental and physical strength that you need to deal with whatever life throws your way.

Myth 2: The goal of the path is to fix ourselves. We typically go in search of spirituality when we are at our lowest points, or at least it was so in my case, and I'm grateful for all the lessons and tools that this path equipped me with. We have to take time to connect with ourselves on a daily basis, to think and reflect on all that we're doing and all that is happening. Some days we may need a little extra space or time to make sense of it all because his path is not some ten-step resource that will magically turn our lives around. The truth is that all the answers we need already exist within us. No one knows us better than ourselves, so listening to our inner voice is how we make our way back home to ourselves.

Myth 3: There's a very specific way to do things. There isn't. The path to happiness, peace, joy, and love are diverse, so the best one is the one that feels good and true to you. Test the waters and find the practices you feel you can integrate well within your day-to-day life.

Myth 4: This one really cracks me up a little—**you turn into one of those people who drink herbal teas and nothing else.** Girl, if you enjoy drinking a cocktail every now and again, please don't let that stop you. Or if coffee is more your jam, don't deny yourself one of life's little joys because someone on Instagram claimed that it's bad for you.

Myth 5: You have to be a religious person. Spirituality should not be confused with religion. I read a profound statement that so succinctly differentiated the two concepts. This statement essentially narrowed it down to religion being about a messenger (God or whomever you choose to believe in) and spirituality being a lot more about following the message. It's about something that is a lot larger than us and learning to express meaning and our connectedness to the now. The beautiful thing about living in a world that has progressed as much as the one we live in is that we have access to a plethora of beliefs. You get to pick where you go and what is right for you.

Exploring Spiritual Self-Care

Learning to incorporate spiritual wellness into your routine is going to be an absolute game-changer for you. And remember, just as with any other self-care practice, it needn't be overly complicated for you.

Here are a few strategies on what you can do to start, remember spiritual wellness has a loud platform so be open to explore and try new things:

✸ **Clean your space.** Our material possessions have energy attached to them, and that is both good and bad energy. So you need to take some time out of your schedule and get rid of those things that you feel no longer fit the life that you are building for yourself at the moment. Start in your closet, and get rid of the clothes that you are no longer wearing or the ones that no longer fit you. Donate them to someone less fortunate or to charity. Then move on over to other miscellaneous items such as books, knick-knacks, or ornaments. I know that we hold on to stuff because we feel guilty that we might need it in the future or because someone gifted it to us, but my words of wisdom are, "If you feel like an item has no value to you, where you are right now, thank it for the purpose that it played in your life and let it go."

✸ **Worship.** I love to worship. I love to sing, read, and talk about the God I serve. He has been good to me, better than I have ever been to myself in this lifetime. He loves me despite all of my shortcomings and mistakes, so if that isn't reason enough to praise and worship him, then I don't know what is. The most common misconception that people have is that worship is something that only takes place in a church building, but that couldn't be further from the truth. It is something that happens in our hearts, our heads, and the space all around us.

❈ **Through music.** Yes, spiritual wellness lives through music we can do two things; worship and praise by listening to and singing songs of praise. I am not the best kind of singer, but that certainly does not stop me from belting loudly. Or songs that sound similar to nature and resemble peace and tranquility they just flow right through you.

❈ **You can listen to an inspirational black speaker.** There is so much wisdom that we can gain from listening to other people speak. The lessons you learn simply because you can relate and they say it how it is. You can also turn to spiritual literature; in the form of fiction or non-fiction books. To me, spiritual books are something that fires up my imagination, stirs my soul, and reminds me of what a great adventure life can be; they are tools that I can use to help those seeds of good within me.

❈ **Be an act of service.** By serving and helping others spiritually, it can be a privilege to be in a position where you are able to help another. When we serve others, it shows how grateful we are for the provision in our lives and the extension of good we can be in this world.

❈ **By living fully and apologetically.** Life is about stewardship, using the talents and gifts that we were given to leave our mark on this earth and inspire. So if you are a writer or an artist, use those talents to spread and share messages about hope. Black women are so used to hearing people tell them they should be subtle, quiet, and reserved about their dreams. So those who use their voice and their gifts as a platform are opening up the arena for their sisters to do the same as well.

❊ **Express love to all other people.** I will admit it's hard to love people at times especially when they've wronged you or treated you unfairly, but sometimes those difficult people are the ones who need light more than we do. So shine that light upon those people, and be a positive influence. It inspires them to be the change that they see in you. Spiritually has no bounds and limits and wraps itself around everybody.

It's in the stories of growth and progress that we share with others. When we take the time to look at the entirety of our lives, we will come to realize that there is really no shortage of miracles and stories that remind us of God's love, grace, and mercy. Worship through storytelling is simply about letting other people know how good God is and how good he can be to them.

Love yourself well. You were created in the image of your creator. So, learn to love yourself and appreciate it more, and be intentional about taking care of your mental, physical, and spiritual health. It's okay if you struggle at times. What matters is the amount of work you put in and the intention and dedication you take.

Spiritual wellness doesn't have a certain aesthetic. Some days it will look like complete stillness and silence. On some other days, it will look a lot louder, like jumping around in your living room. It's messy on some days, with tear-stained pillows and shaky hands, but an incredibly beautiful thing to engage in. It's a poster of the heart and mindset you carry, so I encourage you to seek it in and find the way that feels most authentic and true to you. There was this day—a day I'll never forget—I was through the park and saw what looked to be a group of college students. They all had their Starbucks takeaway coffee mugs at the ready, and there was something else, they had their bibles with them. And then there was this one young lady—I'll never forget her face and the sound of her melodic voice as she pirouetted around those trees and she just sang that she couldn't believe how good her Lord was. At that moment, it didn't matter who was around her or what anyone else thought of her. That is worship at its most authentic. I prayed a little prayer in my heart for her and her friends to never lose that fire for worship within them.

Worship is a place where you feel safe and connect with the presence that you feel—that is what I saw on that day in the park.

Grab a journal and start writing. The act of writing is a sacred one. I know I've mentioned it before but writing is one of the best ways in which we can allow ourselves to process the fullness of our emotions and increase awareness about the things that are troubling us. Journaling, although quite simple, can be quite a difficult process to navigate. For spiritual journalling, follow these simple steps to get started and ease into the process.

✽ Make it easy for yourself. If you prefer using a plain notebook, then that is perfect. You don't have to go buy one of those fancy-looking journals that come with all types of folders and compartments. Simple is okay, and if it works for you, then that's a thousand times better.

✽ If you don't know what to write about, write about gratitude because gratitude never fails us. It's a great way to help you lift your spirits and to remind you of how incredible life can be.

✽ Change up the environment. Putting yourself in an environment you wouldn't normally go into can be helpful. I have found that sitting in a peaceful coffee shop and just writing about everything that has or hasn't been going on is a great way to disengage and detach from life's daily stressors.

✽ Make it personal. Make it messy because no one else has to read it but you. So don't obsess too much about how neat or not neat your handwriting looks. Rather focus on the feeling that the process brings up.

Journal Prompts and Ideas to Get You Started

- *Define what spirituality is and what it means to you.*
- *What adds meaning to your life and leaves you feeling purposeful and content?*
- *During which moments do you tend to feel most connected to your spiritual side?*
- *Make a list of some of the unanswered questions in your life.*
- *Make a list of your favorite ways to spend the hours in your day.*
- *What are the words that you want to live by?*
- *Define what unconditional love looks like for you.*
- *Use 10 words or less to describe what it feels like to be YOU.*
- *Define some of the things you would like to say yes to and the things you want to say no to. In essence, define or describe what your year of YES would look like for you.*

Meditation. If you are looking for a practice that will bring you close to your inner strengths, then this could be a practice that is for you. Besides that, it can potentially reduce your stress and improve your concentration. Similarly, yoga is a popular practice for spiritual self-care too. It can teach you how to breathe and hone in on your inner thoughts and feelings because it quiets the noise, helps you tune in with the rest of your body, and makes you more discerning. You have to be able to choose a technique that feels right for you. We are all different, so we have to shape spiritual self-care to what suits and satisfies us.

Here is a simple breathwork exercise to help you connect to the power of your breath:

Shhh… Just Breathe. Do you ever wonder why people say, "just breathe" when you're in panic mode? It's because breathing brings us closer to us and our bodies. The best part about using breathing as a mindful exercise is that you can do it pretty much anywhere. All you have to do is to focus on your breath for a couple of minutes.

- You start by breathing slowly through your nose and out through your mouth. Try to keep this rhythm and pace for about six seconds.
- Release the burden from your thoughts. That is everything that you are carrying—the things that you still need to do today. The things that you are stressing about. Let it all go, and focus all your attention on the rhythm and the pace of your breathing.
- How does it feel to have the breath move throughout your body and fill you within? Once you and your breath have become one, watch it as it dissipates out into the world.

Remember that if every moment of this exercise was enjoyable for you, you can go on ahead and practice it for as long as you want.

Other connections to spiritual enlightment is;

Awareness. I particularly love this exercise because it teaches us to appreciate the daily tasks that we sometimes label as dull or mundane. Think about those activities that you take for granted. Do you take time to appreciate that you are alive…and still able to enjoy the fruits of the world and everything it provides….the scents you smell, the small movements you make, and even the food you eat? Really soak in everything around you. Do you appreciate how lucky you are? Choose that one thing that you can relate to, and instead of doing that task on autopilot, take the time to bring purposeful awareness into the task. It's going to transform your whole life.

Embracing your ancestral heritage. Think about a tradition that you can engage in to connect with ancient traditions. Or travel to your ancestral homelands to really connect with where you come from, which will open up a world of connectedness and a feeling of belonging that can feel like a spiritual home.

Spending time outside. Gardening is an excellent activity that you can do to keep yourself grounded. You don't have to think about anything. Just focus on the feeling and the peace that it brings you. The things you can touch and appreciate; the spoils of the earth, the grass, the flowers, the sun, the sky the feeling of serenity and the beautiful creations all around us.

Alone Time. We all need our own space from time to time, from partners, kids, family and work. Time to refocus your energy and reboot is crucial. Go for a walk or sit on a park bench and reflect, and pray, even take yourself on a lunch date, do some journaling, breathing exercises, set life goals, recite positive affirmations do what makes you smile in that moment because having your own space is sometimes what our inner crown needs.

AFFIRMATIONS FOR SPIRITUALITY AND PEACE

I am rooted and connected to the abundance that the universe has for me.

I breathe in the light and the peace made by my creator for me.

My happiness comes from understanding that I don't have to have everything figured out on my own.

My spirit is my guide, and I can trust that it is leading me to the exact place where I need to be.

It is well and easy with my soul.

Right now, in this moment, I choose to let go of worry and claim the peace that is rightfully mine.

Faith over perfection and worry. Those are the words that will guide me through this life.

Good things will always find me because the very essence of me is good.

SIX
SOCIAL SELF-CARE

In the moments when it was most difficult for me to breathe or move, it was women who came and stood by my side to lift me up. It was women who cared for and nourished me back to life.

I AM AN INDEPENDENT REBEL. I have always held on to the idea that I don't need anyone or that I do not rely on anyone. So to say I have always been an "I can hold my own" kind of girl. It wasn't until I fell pregnant for the first time that I realized just how important sisterhood and community are. From the beginning, I had my girlfriends to lean on and have honest conversations about my thoughts, feelings, and fears. After giving birth, I had women who stood by me as I healed and my body transitioned. They fed me, and one thing about us black people —we will feed one another. I had women call and reach out to send messages of congratulations and kind words. I can't say that I am an expert at accepting help, but I can say that nowadays, I'm leaving the door slightly ajar and I am not as resistant to help as I was a couple of years ago.

As we start this journey on social self-care and community, these are the words that I would like you to start with:

'**You are not a burden. You're lovable even if you need to be given repeated reassurance. You are lovable even if you have been hurt before by people who you loved and thought loved you back. You are lovable even if you have mental issues and things that you struggle with. You are lovable, even if you feel you aren't deserving of that love. You are lovable regardless of whatever past lies behind you.**'

Human beings are social creatures. We thrive, bloom, and flourish when we are well-loved by those who are closest to us. Love and belonging are fundamental aspects of healthy relationships and can lead to more joy, satisfaction, and fulfillment.

I am grateful for the people in my life. Friends, family, co-workers, and acquaintances are all alike. Somedays, one completely random moment, I will look all around me and think silently to myself, how lucky am I that I get to have these people in my life. It truly is a blessing. *People* are a blessing. As black sisters, we ought to stand together, and I believe that as much as we advocate caring for ourselves, it's just as important that we leave a little room open for one another as well.

Caring for each other as much as we care about ourselves allows us to look at the world from a whole new perspective. We open our eyes up to the 3-dimensions of the world. We may all be black women, but that does not mean that we are the same. We come from different socioeconomic backgrounds, different family dynamics, and different cultures; it's a learning opportunity and an invitation for us to learn more about compassion and empathy. Black comes in various shades, and from where I am standing, that is a rather beautiful sight to see.

FOCUSING ON COMMUNITY SELF-CARE

As black women, the message that *'all we have is each other'* is so regularly reinforced. And as I look back on all that we have survived and endured and have had to fight for, I can't help but be reminded over and over again that we, as black women are the backbone of society, not just as sisters or as mothers or aunts but as friends, teachers and partners too. The one thing that I want all of us to remember, as well, is that our role here on earth is not just to provide or give support but to receive it without ever questioning whether or not we deserve it or not.

The terms "*community*," "*sisterhood*," and "*black empowerment*" are seen almost everywhere. But what do they truly mean to each of us, and why are they so important? I'll start first. To me, it's all about having a circle of trusted people who I can turn to when I am in need of some support or validation. It's a kind of connectedness aligned with the premise of unconditional love. A lack of judgment regardless of my people's shortcomings or mistakes. It's about ensuring that my people are validated and encouraged to live their lives without feeling that they are judged for their decisions. It's having people around me who I know will fix my crown and vice versa. People to laugh out loudly in times of joy. It's truly such a joy and a blessing to be surrounded by people day in and day out who remind you that you are loved and will never have to walk alone.

Through sisterhood and community, we get to learn that family can be found with people who aren't necessarily our blood family. Both connection and sisterhood are about forming meaningful bonds and emotional support, and it's also about being seen, heard, and understood.

It's empowering. Scientists established long ago that community has essential benefits for our health and our wellbeing. Community goes far beyond that, however. It's knowing that we are supported and seen that allows us to stand in our power and claim the divine power that is ours in our own lives.

It's liberating. There is just something about being around a supportive group of people that gives us that feeling of newfound freedom. Over the years, and throughout the process of writing this book, I spent a lot of time talking to black women, and the one thing that many of them used to tell me is that it was so liberating for them to have people to talk to who understand. People who don't try to downplay or diminish their existence. They also expressed their relief that having communities allowed them to shed that belief that black women must be strong all the time; that they can detach from their masculine skins and show up 100% as themselves without judgment or shame.

Community allows us to immerse ourselves in the fullness of our black femininity, and I believe that is a rather beautiful thing. People shine and show up as their best selves when they are seen and acknowledged, so hearing that my black sisters have a platform out there to share their experiences while being validated for it, makes my heart full and overflowing with joy!

Having a community also allows us to expand our horizons and be more considerate in the way we interact with and engage with our people. No two people are ever the same, nor will they ever be the same. Learning to accept, welcome, and embrace each other's unique blackness allows us to form bonds that teach us not to look down on one another.

There is a particular pressure that comes with black women. There's the pressure to have it together all the time, to look after your family while balancing a career where you have to fight three times harder to be seen. In finding our community, we can teach ourselves to be a lot kinder to one another as well.

The power of community

I believe that the right people don't save us, but they walk beside us and hold our hands as we save ourselves. In this heavy world that sometimes seems as if it is devoid of any good, my prayer for you is that you will find your people. The kind of people who hold you quietly as you figure things out. The people who see you and celebrate you. The people who stay with you and watch you grow.

Who are your people, and are you actively working on nurturing those relationships and bringing yourself closer to them? There is so much power in knowing that you do not have to do life alone. You'll become a better person and accomplish things that you never could've imagined yourself accomplishing.

Here are three of my favorite reasons, why I prefer and choose to keep a tight community of people in my life:

1.Wisdom. I don't have all the answers. I don't have it all figured out, but what I do know is that one of my sisters in growth understands and will come to me with the words that I need.

2.Motivation when there is none coming from me. On those days when my motivation isn't doing the things that it needs to be doing, I look all around me at the fierce, hardworking, powerful women around me and become inspired. Those sisters of mine are a reminder that even when it's hard, challenges can be conquered, and victory can be mine.

3.Endless support. We are our worst critics. Sometimes I find myself saying the harshest of things to myself. On those days, I pause a while to think back at what they would say to me and change that inner dialogue. Our people believe in us more than we believe in ourselves—that's why we need to lean on them. They'll always be there to remind us why we need to keep going. To keep pushing.

I believe without a doubt that good people find each other. My hope for you is that when you find those special people for yourself, you allow them to flow right into your life as they are meant to.

Finding Your Community of People

If you're somewhat of an introvert, then the thought of going outside of your comfort zone and actually making the intentional effort to socialize can be anxiety-inducing. But the reality is that it is all about finding the right community of people with whom you can be your very best self around. Let's look at some of the creative ways to enlarge your community and find your tribe of people.

Allow social media to be your voice. I have a love/hate relationship with social media. I love the fact I get to document and show my followers who I truly am and what I believe in. I love the fact that it allows me to advocate and fight for causes that I am passionate about, such as feminism and the #blacklivesmatter movement. I love that it allows me to shed light on the heavy, not-so-easy-to-talk-about topics such as gender and race inequalities. It's a way of letting people know that these issues are real issues affecting real people. On the flip side, it can be a different type of hell because of how careless people have gotten. People think that they are entitled to say anything and everything they want because of their social right to freedom of speech. They use their platforms to spread hate and to break people down. But regardless of those bad apples lurking around in our timelines and our feeds, I still believe that we shouldn't allow them to prevent us from sharing our stories of hope. So, go beyond the hashtag and fight for that cause that you're passionate about.

You can start a blog about parenting for black women, food and wellness, home decor, or simply about you; What being a black woman means to you. You can write about your everyday life experiences. Challenges you face or the misconceptions people have about being a black woman. So many women need to be reminded that their everyday struggles aren't just something they are struggling with. They will be able to find comfort in the fact that someone else shares in and understands their struggles and is working to help them overcome them.

Start your own sisterhood group. We need women as women. Women *who can* lend a hand when we need one. Women *who can* remind us of the light we carry. Women *who can* remind us of our purpose and life's vision. Women *who can* make us accountable to our self-care goals and what better way to do that than through a Black Women's sisterhood group? Start off by looking for a group of women who are just as passionate as you are about starting a group where everyone can channel and cultivate that "yes I am" type of energy. It makes it a safe and positive space. Rather than a negative one. Because I get it sometimes all we wanna do, when we're with our friends is b**** and complain, but in all honesty, that kind of energy is really bad for us and our wellbeing. We can't always be expected to fix or have solutions to our friends' problems. That is why it's important to ensure we don't allow negative feelings to dominate our relationships.

Commit to buying from a black-owned business to support those black business in the community. As we learn to love ourselves, we need to learn and to trust in our black businesses too. As we cultivate the love for our people, drop the judgement or critical shield and pour into them, as you do yourself. Not all businesses have it put together, as they may be building on their organisation as you are building on you. We have enough hate in the world to project it on our own. If they thrive, we thrive as well as does the next generation. Maybe volunteer your services, your support because its opening up opportunities for yourself that you would have maybe closed off.

Make time for your sisterhood. I don't mean to get together every weekend, just remain intentional about keeping in touch with one another. Send inspirational text messages. Remember the important things that are happening in their lives. Reach out and ask for help if you need it. Involve them and be involved in their lives as well; sisterhood is such a remarkable thing.

Leverage your interests. Be loud and unapologetic about the things that interest you and set your soul on fire. The best thing about technology is that it has made it seemingly more accessible to find people who are interested in similar niches as we are. There are Facebook groups that are available for you to join, and if you ever feel like you can't find what you are looking for, you can move on over and use a site such as meet up to organize a gathering of your own.

Support a black activist group. With so much noise going on around us and racial discrimination being at the forefront of some of this, having that community can sometimes feel like a safe haven. You don't have to throw yourself in deep, but if there is a petition you feel passionate about or a topic that will rally a positive light or fire in you join and show support. The sheer feeling that you are part of something important, is a great way to boost your mental state, because it is purposeful and fulfilling and a great way to celebrate unity and belonging when you feel alone.

Check out a new restaurant with some of your friends. Food is a central theme in African culture. It's also a great way that we can learn more about our friends, where they come from, and the history behind their favorite foods.

Try group therapy. If you are thinking of giving therapy a go, but aren't too convinced by the whole idea of sitting and having a one on one with someone that you barely know, then group therapy might just be for you. Getting help while still being surrounded by people who are facing similar changes can help enforce that sense of community and support.

Plan a girls holiday. No matter who you are…..we all love a holiday. To be able to stop, take a break and relax is everyone's ideal situation. A holiday with family or children is slightly different as we still tend to take that 'superwomen cape' away with us and often come back feeling more tired. So find some friends or a group of black women who love travelling and just go away. You don't always have to plan it months in advance, have a checklist in place, or it be top-of-the-range luxurious; learn to let go and enjoy yourself. To just get away from it all, and do you for a few days with like-minded women is sometimes its own true therapy.

Community, friendship, and sisterhood as a whole are there to remind us of our sister's incredible contributions. Throughout history, black women have shaped the human experience and culturally transformed our world, so our connection to one another is one of the ways through which we can honor those achievements. But it still is an opportunity for us to consider and think about how much further we still need to and can go along because the denial of black women and their rights is still a grave injustice.

I am constantly and always in awe of the women in my life. The women I have met in the church, at work, in the lines at the coffee shop during my early morning coffee runs, and the women I am tied to by blood. I am in awe of all they are doing and are still going to do. However we can sometimes be our own worst enemies by knocking ourselves down as a community and not pledging that 'community bond' or holding that flag up high. Not coming together as we should stems from years and years and years of oppression and how we view ourselves as people, but the more we come together as one, one voice, and one community and hold each other up, the more we'll see the next generation follow on from what they see and learn from it. So we should never stop rooting for and advocating for each other.

Ways to Nurture Your Relationships

Having genuine connections with people is such a blessing, and that is why we should never stop reminding those people how grateful we are for having them in our lives. Here are a few final words and suggestions on how you can continue to show up for your tribe and how you can love them better.

Express gratitude. "Thank you for the coffee. Thank you for the sweet text message that you left me. Thank you for being there when I need you. Thank you for being you and for allowing me to be me." These are simple words that will help a person understand that they are more than just "a person" or an acquaintance, but that they hold a valuable position in your life.

Be honest. As much as we choose to be honest with them about what we love about them, we also have to be brave enough to let them know when they are doing things they don't like. Perhaps you don't like the fact that they are always late for your coffee meet-ups. Tackle that point of frustration rather than letting that valuable friendship waste away. There might be something happening in their lives, or maybe things haven't been going all that well.

Friendships also require some work, so you'll know that if things don't work out at some point, you'll know that you tried.

Encourage their dreams. Did your girl just let you in on a secret about a new business venture that she's taking up, or did she just tell you about a boss career move that she is going to make? Show her that you believe in her and her dream by offering support in any way or form.

Be loyal. Don't do things to them that you wouldn't appreciate them doing to you. In other words, don't talk behind their back or try to sabotage their dreams because you envy them. If you have an issue with them, approach them directly, and if you feel that it's time to let go of the friendship, go ahead. Sometimes friendships end—it's a part of the circle of life—and that, too, is okay.

My heart really does go out to those queens who do not compete with one another. The queens who intentionally go out of their way to make their sisters feel seen and heard. The ones who uplift and light each other's spirits. May we be them and always embody that kind of energy.

AFFIRMATIONS FOR COMMUNITY

The presence of others brings me joy because they inspire me to look at life through that of hope and light.

People are a gift. I am grateful for those very good ones that I have in my life.

I will be kind, loving, and considerate to both family and friends.

I speak life into the spirit of all those who are a part of my life. May they be protected and held because they're so valuable to me.

I am blessed and surrounded by people who love me and would fight for me.

I am blessed because I have a community of people who can help me celebrate my aliveness.

SEVEN
PROFESSIONAL SELF-CARE

It shouldn't be an all-or-nothing type of situation. If your job doesn't provide you with some form of joy or space to breathe, you should know that you should take it upon yourself to make that happen for YOU. It's a matter of finding opportunities within that state of busyness.

I DON'T THINK MOST of y'all know this, but professional self-care is something that needs to be practiced too. I get that your job is your livelihood and all, but if it's costing you your mental health and wellness, you have to step back and ask yourself if it truly is all worth it.

Self-care should not just be a part of our personal lives. Taking care of ourselves in the workplace is just as important as well; because if you look at it, the biggest portion of our day is spent at work. So if you aren't intentional about creating healthier work habits for yourself, then the stress that comes from being in an unhealthy work environment is going to seep into other areas of your life as well.

Here are some reasons why taking care of yourself at work will lead you to greater success.

Optimum productivity comes when you are both physically and mentally alert. Think about it this way; your car does not run when your fuel tank is empty, so why would you expect yourself to operate while running on empty? Workplace self-care allows you to effectively manage and balance your workload so that you don't end up overworked, burnt out, and miserable.

Self-care keeps you vibrant and alive, which can result in more creativity and passion for your job. The one thing that I have noticed about me is that my best and most brilliant ideas come when I have recharged and rested sufficiently. I think of it as my body and brain rewarding me and saying 'thank you' for that opportunity to recharge. If you're worn out and exhausted, you start doing things for the sake of doing them, not because you're passionate or interested in them. Exhaustion limits us and our potential, so that's why it's important for us to know where we need to draw the lines and determine for ourselves how much work is too much work.

Also, **self-care is what keeps us in love with ourselves, so therefore professional self-care is what keeps us in love with our jobs.** As a writer, I believe that when I create, write, and share my work from a place of joy and authenticity, my audience picks up on that energy. So when you do your work from a place of excitement, that joy and passion are going to help you as you navigate the next task or project that you need to do. It's the fuel that will sustain you as you navigate your professional life.

I was having a conversation with someone, and they said something that I don't think I'll ever forget. They told me that if you are in a professional setting with weak or nonexistent boundaries, then other people will simply not know how to treat you. People will take advantage of that, or your kind nature and willingness to always help. You're going to start questioning yourself, your potential, and your capabilities. You'll start asking yourself why people are treating you the way they're treating you. Your professional boundaries are a way of letting people know that "this is how I want to be treated" and "this is what I will and will not tolerate, respectfully." So, girl, take that lunch break, leave work when you're actually supposed to leave, and make sure you use your PTO. When you agreed to take that job in exchange for pay and benefits, you did not sign up to sell every moment of your personal time.

Professional self-care encompasses financial self-care to me, they come hand-in-hand. We work to earn money, but when we earn that money we need to be smart with it. Money is a status symbol and has been used to oppress people, divide countries and is the key contributor to the large disproportion of inequality in and around our communities.

A lack of money is one of the lead causes to depression and mental health issues, hence why we need to prioritise our own financial futures and cultivate a healthy money mindset. Setting goals and making plans to establish healthier money habits to build your wealth are small steps to financial empowerment.

Here are 3 simple financial tips to help on your way if you know you need it:

1. Set goals, look at your finances whatever the amount, you can always set money goals for your short term and long term. With the right plan, there is no reason why you can't get there. Valid, they all depend on your individual circumstances so do be open-minded, strict and realistic with what is right for you, so you're motivated to achieve them.

2. Be more accountable, make a budget, pay your bills on time and pay off debts. We need to make our money work for us rather than visa versa. So utilise where your money goes and what you are using it for. Be clear with your intentions and avoid any unnecessary spending and splurging on things you don't need. I'm going to honest this is hard y'all even for me, as I buy allot of stuff, but I know that I don't need them. So it is being intentional with your money and tracking where all your money goes.

3. You can use an app or even journalling to help you log your monthly spends (i.e. income and expenses) and strengthen your relationship with your money. Knowledge is power so understand where your money goes, so you can start to save and invest towards your goals and begin to smash it.

THE LIVES OF WORKING BLACK WOMEN

Being a black woman in a corporation, or any working environment, is a tough task. There are so many unspoken rules. Besides the fact that we have to work 10x harder than everyone around us, there are still those silent, unspoken rules that exist amongst us; but if there is one thing that I must say about us as black women, it's that we will show up and shine in whatever we are doing–at work and otherwise, regardless of the fact that we rarely ever get the recognition and acknowledgment that we truly deserve.

Some of the realities of me being a black woman navigating the workplaces that are predominantly white are:

● We don't want to take up too much space. We don't want to draw too much attention to ourselves. So what we do is try to make our hair and clothing as subtle as possible because we don't want to show off our curves because we assume that it's going to contribute to other people's discomfort.

● You teach yourself to be invisible. Above all, we choose to prioritize the comfort of our white colleagues, and because of this, we find ourselves being walked over or our ideas being ignored.

● People tell you to dim your light. As we mentioned above, it's not uncommon for us to be made to feel as if we are making other people uncomfortable. Especially when the group of people we work with look nothing like us. So many times, we hold back on being our authentic selves so we result to 'code-switching' basically adjusting our speech, behaviour, and cultural expression because we fear that not being accommodating in that sense might make our chances of career advancement a lot less. I can't count how many times I was told to smile because it would make me look a lot friendlier or more approachable. Another habit I have noticed is that I typically wait until everyone else has already spoken to provide any input. I always used to think that it was just because how I was raised, but as I grew older, I recognised that it was mainly because I didn't want to come across as that bossy black woman. Then it dawned on me that I can't 'wholeheartedly' be myself at work, in order to maintain that perception of professionalism and without realising downplay my social cultural standing just to *'fit in'*. Which can sometimes generate subconscious hostility, be exhausting and foster that lack of long-term commitment to the workplace.

❁ You feel like you have to fight the battle all on your own. I don't think there is anybody really there to advocate for black women in the workplace, especially if you're working in a predominantly white environment. There's no person to help you fight for that raise you know you deserve or all of the other equal opportunities your white counterparts get. If you have no one else in your corner who's got your back and is willing to fight for you, it's going to be a sad, sad situation.

❁ Try to break the 'glass ceiling' of advancement to senior leadership roles, we often get overlooked which creates this invisible glass barrier, denying us those top senior positions. Even though we are more than capable and qualified to do so, in a male dominated organisation this conscious or unconscious bias still exists.

So, we are rarely represented in those levels and it remains a constant obstacle and perpetuating cycle. We don't just get judged based on our_work performance, and that is something that's mentally, emotionally, and physically draining.

It's not easy being a woman, more so a black determined-to-thrive independent woman in the workplace who has a multitude of other obstacles that she has to get through to get to that place in her career where she is happy, healthy, and thriving. The question I think that most of us should be asking is: What can we do to support black women in the workplace? I'll start here and advocate this to your work colleagues.

We can start talking about issues such as belonging. Listen, no one wants to feel like they are a diversity hire. *'The token black person'*. So, make us feel seen, heard, and understood. By having someone who will be there to listen to our concerns, and ideas. Someone to help validate our presence in the office. Respect our boundaries and give us the same and equal opportunities that our other colleagues get. Having an ally, a friend, and a support system allows us to be authentically us. Not some makeshift version that they want us to be. So most importantly we need you to…….

1. Listen. Don't brush a black woman off when she is giving off valuable feedback or suggestions. They are in the position that they are in because they have valuable insights and wisdom to offer, and make sure that you follow through on the request as well.

2. Be sensitive when it comes to matters of our hair. In other words, don't police us over what we should or should not do when it comes to our hair.
3. Allow us to be ourselves. Our ancestors did not have the privileges that we have today. So let us show up authentically in all our glory, accept our cultural names and pronunciations so that we can do the very best that we are capable of doing.
4. Be transparent about the pay structures and how they work. It's no secret. Women in the workplace don't get what our male counterparts do for the same job.

Saying No in the Workplace

'May you love yourself enough to know when your boundaries need to be enforced'.

Saying no in the workplace is a valuable skill. It prevents you from loading your plate and your schedule with unnecessary commitments and chaos—this can help you manage workplace burnout, stay on track with your goals, as well as deliver better quality work. We often associate the word no with so much negativity, and that is why we're so hesitant about it, but the good news is that it is possible to know how to say it. The trick is simply to know when and how to say it. Here's your go-to guide that you can refer to when looking to set healthy boundaries for yourself at work.

Know what your needs are. You first have to understand what your needs are in order for you to understand how it is that you can have a healthier environment for yourself. And once you have established this, you need to start evaluating the reasons why these boundaries are important to you. In doing this, you will be able to assert yourself and communicate with confidence should you be met with any pushback.

Practice what you are going to say. If you're still a newbie at the whole setting boundaries concept, then stepping back and relaying to yourself what it is that you want to say will help you build the confidence that you need to articulate your needs with confidence to your employer.

Transparency is key. Your manager or your employer cannot help you if they're only given an embellished version of the story. Be absolutely clear on what you want, what you need, and how you think they can make adjustments to help meet your needs. It might be a scary conversation to have, but it will be worth it.

Small Ways to Set Boundaries at Work

- Informing your colleagues during the times when you will be out of the office and not be taking any work calls or messages
- Following through with your promise by not checking any work-related emails or messages when you are at home

- Not requesting any meeting requests during after hours
- Creating a work environment that allows you to be your best product self, in other words, turning on your headphones when you need to or putting up a Do Not Disturb (DND) sign near your office door or in an area at your workspace that is visible for everyone
- Negotiating and delegating tasks when necessary
- Saying no to the things that are outside your scope of work

Workplace Boundary-Setting Statements

Sometimes I get tongue-tied, especially when I have to do something as hard and uncomfortable as setting a new boundary, but I am sure that it happens to the best of us. So maybe you're still learning to grow the language to stand your own ground when it comes to the workplace. Just like in all the other chapters, I want you to know that I've got you covered.

Here are a few words that can help you find your rhythm and flow in the scheme of things:

❊ You're about to leave for work, and someone asks you to "quickly" help them take a look over a few things; this is what you can say: "I've worked my hours for the day and am wrapping things up, but I am happy to have a chat about that during business hours tomorrow."

❁ You get asked to take on a project while you're still busy with another: "I am still busy with another project of my own right now. I can help you or look at it as soon as I finish this."

❁ It's the weekend, or you're taking a couple of days off to attend to personal matters: "I will be out of the office for (x amount of days); please have any queries forwarded to another department (or include the relevant person's name), or I will gladly look over things when I return to the office again."

A small reminder for you: if you really do not know how or when to even begin setting your boundaries, think critically about what you need or what needs to be done, and then start implementing small boundaries that you have all the influence over. So modify the workflow to something that feels more manageable for you.

- Inform your team about how it is that you prefer to receive requests.
- Add an hour of uninterrupted time to your week.
- Limit your 'yeses' to the things that most excite the hell out of you and contribute to your overall wellbeing at work.

This last bit is also for those sisters who are killing it in the entrepreneurial game: you may be running your own business, which is an incredible thing, but remember that 'you' are, first and foremost, the most important business that you have. The business can't function effectively if you are also not working on yourself. Being an entrepreneur is emotionally drawing, and to ensure that you continue to fall in love with what you do, you must have firm boundaries with your clients and yourself.

Client boundaries; clarify how much you expect to get paid for the service you're rendering. It's pushing back on unreasonable boundaries. Setting expectations about communication too. And having systems in place that support your wellness.

Don't feel you have to do it all. Set days and times in the week to focus on work and to focus on you.

Be consistent with it. The more you stick with a regular routine, the more you are likely to keep doing it. Since you set the rules; have a morning routine before you start working on your business the golden rule could be spend 5-10 minutes doing a quick physical movement followed by professional self care affirmations that I've got for you at the ready just below; to allow you confirm your worth and give you that motivation you need to jump start the day with your head held high with a great sense of achievement at even being at the point where you are, amongst all the struggles and hurdles I know you've had to face along the way. Most black-owned businesses suffer the same challenges of being overshadowed by white-owned businesses. It's hard to stand out, so we have to support one another but not suffer burnout in the process.

Network with like-minded black women in business, join a group and get that community love we need by standing together as one, to uplift the sister entrepreneurs or sister side hustlers in all of us.

AFFIRMING YOUR BOUNDARIES

There's that little part of our brains that will somehow always manage to make us feel as if what we feel or what we want does not matter. Oh, but sis! Affirmations are there to remind us that you count. Your needs count. That you don't have to be a people pleaser all the time. Space is something that we all need. Put these reminders on your desk or in your car to remember that you are not wrong for feeling this way:

Creating boundaries around my work prevents burnout.

I am allowed to say no at work. I am still valuable when I say no to certain projects.

My entire identity does not have to be built around the work that I do.

It's up to me to do the work and to take care of myself. To draw lines where I need to and to find those things that bring me joy.

I love the person I am and will become when I set good and healthy boundaries with myself and others around me.

I can be strong and stand in my own truth without making others feel less than others or shut out.

I must continue to do what I am doing to keep my light shining and iridescent.

I am allowed to voice my own needs when I need to. I choose to honor that balance of give and take in this life.

EIGHT
ENVIRONMENTAL SELF-CARE (SUSTAINING A HEALTHY LIFE AROUND YOU)

Everything that you keep around you should be an extension of who you are and what you are becoming.

DID you know that being around you in your home influences your mood and your spirit the whole day? That is why we must work as hard as possible to create homes and environments for ourselves that improve our energy, not diminish it. We spend a lot of time in our homes, and after we've worked the whole day, the only thing we need is to come home to a place that says: *Welcome. Your soul is safe here with me.* So, let me ask you, is the space around you giving you energy and vitality for life, or is it draining and dragging you down? The smallest changes are often the ones that can help us make our spaces more nurturing for us again.

Let's take a moment to talk about clutter and its overall impact on our environment and its effects on our mental health.

Our mental health is directly linked to and impacted by our physical spaces. A lot of times, it is quite obvious, but on most occasions, it rarely ever is so. You see, when clutter accumulates, we often feel stressed and scatter-brained—the things we're looking for seem much more impossible to locate—and that makes us agitated and short-tempered. The other areas of our lives can slowly start to feel as if they are unraveling, as well. Clutter is a thief that just takes and takes, and these are the things that it's taking from you:

It takes away every bit of contentment that you're capable of experiencing. Here's the thing, when your space (especially your home) is filled with a lot of unnecessary items, your home starts to become a major source of stress for you rather than a sanctuary that you can turn to. So instead of thinking to yourself, "Oh yes! I get to go home to a great space," it turns into a matter of "Do I really need to go to that place?" It gnaws away at the immense pleasure that one gets from being in your space of welcome.

It interferes with the relationships that you have as well. How is that, you ask? It's a pretty simple explanation: when you have too much stuff or too much going on around you in general, you spend the great majority of your time trying to piece and put all of that together. Therefore, it becomes increasingly difficult to focus on and give your people the attention and love that they deserve.

There's also a fierce sense of shame amongst us when it comes to having a space that is filled with a lot of "stuff." When we feel that way, it makes us not want to invite anyone over to our homes which can further impact the relationships that we are building with our friends and family.

Clutter takes away from us that feeling of control that we have over our own lives. You may experience those feelings of utter defeat when you stop to look all around you. Feeling negative about your ability to change the situation around you will leave you feeling hopeless, so you end up not doing anything. You let the stuff build up more and more until it gets worse than it was initially.

This planet, this earth, this place is everything that is here to keep us alive. The food that we eat is grown in its rich soil. The air we breathe comes from the trees that thrive. Its solid ground is where we build the shelters for ourselves that we call home. That's why I want to highlight it as well and shed light on the fact that environmental self-care goes far beyond the clutter in our homes. It's about being intentional in our endeavors to care for and respect our planet as much as possible. Our planet is our home, and if we aren't taking care of it, what other place are we going to have to live? Where are our children and their children going to live?

Taking care of nature—the open space around us—is how we take care of ourselves. The more intentional and committed we can be too loving it well and taking better care of it, the fewer difficulties we'll have in creating surroundings for ourselves that contribute to these beautiful lives of ours.

BEYOND THE CLUTTER: CREATING AN ENVIRONMENT THAT YOU LOVE

Home is where all of the wholeness is. Home is where we rest, recharge, and refuel our spirits. Home is where our hearts are. I'm a firm believer that less is more. I do believe that there is joy in the small, simple things. Simple decor, simple meals, simple moments, and slow, sweet, unhurried conversations. That is where the magic is.

What would you say if I asked you this question: *what is it that I need to let go of*? Look around, and don't worry too much if you don't necessarily have the answer to that question because I've got just the tips you need to help you achieve that goal.

Clear the clutter. Look, I am in no way a minimalist. But that doesn't mean that I don't love having a tidy home. The main goal for me is to have all the things that I like, the things that matter and mean something to me, while things remain as neat and tidy as possible. This is how I achieve that.

❊ Start by removing the 'unnecessary.' I love to shop, but for things I don't necessarily need. The problem with this is that it causes an influx of possessions in our homes and causes a whole lot of unnecessary clutter. To slow this process down, start evaluating your purchases. Ask yourself: do I need this item? Is there a place and a purpose for this thing here? Did I buy this, or am I buying this for all the right reasons?

❊ I'm sure that everything has a place of its own. Most clutter is a result of things lying randomly all around. When you know that all the items in your home have a designated place for them, it'll be a lot easier for you to maintain that order in your home.

❊ Keep a donation pile. These could be the items of clothing that no longer fit you or the kids or the things that you no longer use anymore. There is always someone out there who could use the things that we no longer find handy.

✢ Clean as you go. Doing this not only makes your life easier, but it will certainly ensure that your space remains as clutter-free as possible for the longest time.

✢ Decorate your spaces in a way that feels true and real to you. It's your home. Make it as cozy as you want. It's your place of welcome. Designed to make you feel safe, secure, and content. Here's how you can make that happen.

✢ Cozy seating. Chunky scatter cushions are such a great way to incorporate that extra texture. So add a couple of those to your couch and favorite seating area.

✢ Natural lighting. You want a whole lot of natural light to filter in throughout the day, so make sure that you keep your curtains open throughout the day to ensure that the room remains as welcoming as possible.

✢ Make the rooms smell lovely. Open windows do wonders for allowing a lot of fresh air to come in through the room. You can also make or purchase home fragrances to ensure your space smells fresh and clean.

For as much as you can, opt for the use of natural, toxin-free products by making your own. There are tons of solutions that you can make using simple household ingredients such as vinegar, lemon, and baking soda. This not only protects the environment but also helps to reduce your exposure to harmful products as much as possible.

Try spending more time in nature so that you can connect to the world around you. This practice goes perfectly hand in hand with spiritual self-care. So you can use the time as well to engage in a little bit of prayer or to meditate on truth and peace.

Do an observation exercise. This is a pretty simple exercise that is there to help you notice and appreciate more of your surroundings. It is there to help keep you anchored to all the natural beauty that surrounds you—something that we so often take for granted and overlook all so easily.

❊ Find any object in the environment that you're in. It could be a flower, a vase, or a rock. Keep your attention focused solely on this object for about a minute or two. Concentrate on this object for as long as your mind allows. Look at it from the eyes of a child, with awe and excitement. Immerse yourself in its presence and connect with the purpose that it serves.

❊ Go to the beach. Spend time by the sea. I love the sounds of the waves. Doesn't everyone? Feet in the sand and reflecting on life can be true therapy. The fresh air in our lungs and that connectedness with nature are all we need to feel whole sometimes.

AFFIRMATIONS FOR A PEACEFUL ENVIRONMENT

Everything is energy. Therefore I am going to make sure that I create and cultivate a peaceful environment all around me.

Every breath I take is an invitation for peace to enter and reside in my body.

I am mindful of the energy that I allow into my space. My peace is non-negotiable, so I will strive to create a life that is serene, harmonious, and fulfilling.

Peace and progress are my main priorities.

Even when the world around me seems to be coming apart at the seams, I will remain grounded and rooted.

I will allow myself the pleasure of slowing down and enjoying the state of the world around me as it is.

NINE
CELEBRATING PROGRESS AND MAKING SELF-CARE A LIFELONG JOURNEY

If you're walking along the right path and will yourself to keep walking, even when things get hard, you'll win and make it to the finish line.

LIKE I'VE SAID, self-care is a forever journey. It's not just about the aesthetics, the bubble baths, or the aromatherapy. That's just a short-term fix. We are in it for the long haul. It's about accountability. Putting yourself first, prioritizing you, and setting those healthy boundaries. It's also getting to the root cause of your issues and processing your trauma so that you don't have to relive it for the rest of your life. It's not going to be easy, but it's worth it. Sis, I want you to remember that because our journey together is now coming to an end, it doesn't mean that you have to stop here as well. I hope you take tomorrow and the rest of the days after that to continue working on and bettering yourself. Just in case it gets a little hard, here are a few final tips for you for every day of the week:

Tip 1: Release all expectations. There's no right or wrong way to care for yourself, so go ahead and do what feels most nourishing to your body and spirit. You don't have to place unnecessary pressure on yourself.

Tip 2: Fresh air is always a winner. Lace up your shoes for a lap or a walk around the block or just open up your window and simply enjoy a gulp of fresh air. It can be revitalizing.

Tip 3: Do make time to socialize. People are important, and having a social life becomes much more pleasant and easier when we know that we don't have to go at it alone.

Tip 4: Remove the superwoman cape. Stop trying to do it all or have it all figured out on your own. There's no shame in allowing yourself to be helped. In fact, it will make you a greater and even more spectacular you.

Tip 5: Have better and stronger boundaries. Say no more often to other people, but yes to you more often. You don't have to overextend yourself to be liked or accepted. You are enough as you are. Your heart is enough as it is. You're loved here. You're accepted here. You're wanted here as you are.

Tip 6: Work on having healthier coping mechanisms. When challenges arise, you have to know how you're going to meet them.

Tip 7: Rest. Rest your mind, your body, and your spirit. There's no guilt or shame in not being productive. To be here, present, and fully alive, we must embrace that sweetness of doing nothing.

There are a multitude of things that you're going to have to work on in this lifetime, but the fact that you are worth it and enough as you are doesn't have to be one of those things. The kind of energy that I want you to carry with you is one that says, "I'm worth it." This is the kind of energy that is open to freedom. It's the energy of doing things that align with your spirit and your soul. Again, I'm not saying that it's going to be a breeze or smooth sailing all along the way because it isn't, but it's so incredibly worth it—self-work always is. So show up; show up messily and afraid with a brave but hopeful heart. You owe it to yourself to write that story of how you lived your life fully.

Place your hands on your heart and repeat after me…

I LOVE being a black woman. I am beautiful, I am loved and capable of setting my own path and pushing forward with my dreams by making a radical change to invest in myself, and I wouldn't want to be anything or anyone else but me.

YOUR CHANCE TO HELP SOMEONE DIFFERENTIATE BETWEEN SELF-CARE AND SELFISHNESS

You should have all the tools and resources you need to know about prioritizing your physical, mental, emotional, and spiritual well-being.

The next step is simple… by leaving your honest opinion of this book on Amazon, you can show other black women how to pursue the joy that is our birthright. This is our space to show up authentically, and be advocates for self-care. So share what you have learnt, so we can grow and heal as black women together—this is the time we need to show up for one another.

Thank you for your help. As a collective, we should now empower other black women to understand that the deepest love begins within… As I pass the baton… do your bit… It's that easy. **https://geni.us/selfcare_review**

Scan the QR code to leave a review or visit the link above!

CONCLUSION

Dear Black Girl,

I hope that you continue to choose yourself.

I hope you continue to commit to making your life as beautiful and peaceful as ever.

Sis, I pray that you never stop validating yourself. Whatever you are looking for in this life, I hope that you give yourself full permission to have those things. Because when you do, I promise you, the world will open up in a way that you never imagined possible.

It may feel overwhelming for you at first, but remember that this is a journey that is taken in small steps. So look daily for those small things that you can do for yourself. Go all in and continue to create that life that feels most aligned and true to you. Take your heart and pour it into your whole way of living.

CONCLUSION

Even though this is the end of our journey together, I want you to remember that I will always be here for you, rooting and championing you.

This is to us.

To our melanin.

And to thriving.

You are a crown of beauty.

Take care, sis.

ABOUT THE AUTHOR

Helene A. Waigo is a wife and mother to three beautiful children. As a dynamic author Helene has become a self-care advocate for black women. Being a black woman herself, Helene understands the unique struggles and challenges that Black women face in modern society today, when it comes to prioritizing their wellbeing.

Drawing from her own personal experiences and stories of black women that she has worked with over the years. Helene's mission is to champion, inspire and motivate black women to take control of their health and happiness, with easy-to-implement tools and resources to help them feel empowered, heal from negative past traumas and be confident in their self-care journey.

Her contagious energy and passion for self-care have made her put all she has learnt into her book ''A Crown of Beauty – Self-care for Black Women' so it becomes the go-to resource for black women looking to improve their mental and emotional wellbeing to inspire them on their journey to self-discovery, healing and personal growth across all areas of their lives.

REFERENCES

AARP. (n.d.). *Skin-Care Tips From Black Women Dermatologists*. AARP. https://www.aarp.org/entertainment/style-trends/info-2022/skin-care-tips-from-black-women-dermatologists.html

American Academy of Dermatology. (n.d.). *Black hair: Tips for everyday care*. Www.aad.org. https://www.aad.org/public/everyday-care/hair-scalp-care/hair/care-african-american

Black Ballad. (2021, March 2). *We Need An Honest Conversation About Black Women, Families & Boundaries*. Black Ballad. https://blackballad.co.uk/views-voices/we-need-an-honest-conversation-about-black-women-families-boundaries?listIds=605376e5f24df005d63304c7

Bryant, T. (2022, February 9). *10 Biggest Barriers To Black Mental Health Today*. Psycom.net https://www.psycom.net/black-mental-health-barriers

Charles, C. (2023, February 9). *Barriers often keep Black community from seeking help for mental health*. The Hill. https://thehill.com/changing-america/well-being/mental-health/3851566-barriers-often-keep-black-community-from-seeking-help-for-mental-health/

Davis, F. (n.d.). 11 Spiritual Self Care Ideas to Ignite Your Inner Spirit. Cosmic Cuts. Retrieved March 19, 2023, from https://cosmiccuts.com/blogs/healing-stones-blog/spiritual-self-care-ideas

Dhu, P. (2020, January 21). *Why Setting Boundaries Is Important In The Workplac*e Violet Dhu. Corporate Communication Experts. https://corporatecommunicationexperts.com.au/setting-boundaries-in-the-workplace/

Dreeben, O. (2001). *Health Status of African Americans*. Journal of Health & Social Policy, 14(1), 1–17. https://doi.org/10.1300/j045v14n01_01

Essence. (n.d.-a). B*lack Women at Work: How We Shape Our Identities On the Job*. Essence. https://www.essence.com/news/money-career/black-women-work-how-we-shape-our-identities-job/

Essence. (n.d.-b). *Protect Your Magic! 9 Self Care Acts Black Women Should*

REFERENCES

Practice Daily. Essence. https://www.essence.com/lifestyle/health-wellness/9-self-care-tips-black-women-should-practice-daily/

Everyday Health. (2020, November 12). *6 Black Influencers to Follow for Healthy-Eating Inspiration*. EverydayHealth.com. https://www.everydayhealth.com/diet-nutrition/black-influencers-to-follow-for-healthy-eating-inspiration/

For Harriet. (2016, September 16). *Self-Preservation as Self-Care: How to Set Healthy Boundaries*. For Harriet I Celebrating the Fullness of Black Womanhood. http://www.forharriet.com/2015/09/self-preservation-as-self-care-how-to.html

Gillette, B. (2021, March 6). *Skincare Tips for BIPOC Women*. The Everygirl. https://theeverygirl.com/skincare-tips-for-black-and-brown-women/

Glowiak, M. (2020, April 14). *What is Self-Care and Why is it Important For You?* Www.snhu.edu. https://www.snhu.edu/about-us/newsroom/health/what-is-self-care

Harbinger, J. (2022, April 25). *8 Signs It's Time to Cut a Toxic Person Out of Your Life (And How to Do It)*. Jordan Harbinger. https://www.jordanharbinger.com/8-signs-its-time-to-cut-a-toxic-person-out-of-your-life-and-how-to-do-it/

Harvard School of Public Health. (2019, July 2). *Vitamin D*. The Nutrition Source. https://www.hsph.harvard.edu/nutritionsource/vitamin-d/

Health, C. (n.d.). *7 Common Health Concerns African Americans Should Monitor - CentraState Healthcare System*. CentraState Health Care System. https://www.centrastate.com/blog/7-common-health-concerns-african-americans-should-monitor/

Jed Foundation. (n.d.). *How to Take Care of Yourself While Taking Care of Friends*. The Jed Foundation. https://jedfoundation.org/resource/how-to-take-care-of-yourself-when-youre-taking-care-of-friends/

Kindelan, K. (n.d.). *Listen to Michelle Obama's self-care message: Why women need to put themselves first*. Good Morning America. https://www.goodmorningamerica.com/wellness/story/listen-michelle-obamas-care-message-women-put-64189509

Lutz, R. (2017). Health Disparities Among African-Americans I Pfizer.

REFERENCES

Pfizer.com. https://www.pfizer.com/news/articles/health_disparities_among_african_americans

Mint Life. (2021, May 17). *Don't Lose Money to Burnout by Setting Boundaries at Work.* MintLife Blog. https://mint.intuit.com/blog/remote-work/setting-boundaries-at-work/

Modern Therapy. (2015, October 25). *8 Areas of Self-Care.* Modern Therapy. https://moderntherapy.online/blog-2/areas-of-self-care

Muck, P. (2021, September 14). *The Benefits of Yoga: How It Boosts Your Mental Health.* Www.houstonmethodist.org. https://www.houstonmethodist.org/blog/articles/2021/sep/the-benefits-of-yoga-how-it-boosts-your-mental-health/

Nast, C. (2022, June 12). *Why Is Exhaustion So Normalized for Black Women?* Allure. https://www.allure.com/story/black-women-rest-self-care

Natural Girl Wigs. (n.d.). *20 Ways To Care For Your Afro Textured Hair.* Natural Girl Wigs. https://naturalgirlwigs.com/blogs/beauty/how-to-care-for-your-natural-hair

O'Brien, A. (2020, October 15). *Environmental Self-Care: Self-Care Series (Part 5).* Oregon Counseling. https://oregoncounseling.com/article/environmental-self-care/

Oregon Counselling. (2020, October 15). *Environmental Self-Care: Self-Care Series (Part 5).* Oregon Counseling. https://oregoncounseling.com/article/environmental-self-care/

Perry, E. (2022, August 25). *How To Set Boundaries at Work: A Personal Guide to Drawing the Line.* Betterup https://www.betterup.com/blog/how-to-set-boundaries-at-work

Sander, L. (2019). *What does clutter do to your brain and body?* NewsGP. https://www1.racgp.org.au/newsgp/clinical/what-does-clutter-do-to-your-brain-and-body

Sisters. (2022, October 4). *40 Foods Every Black Woman Over 40 Should Consider Eating.* Sisters. https://www.sistersletter.com/health/40-foods-every-black-woman-over-40-should-consider-eating

Spiritual Club. (2017, September 5). *Spiritual Self-Care Activities* Spiritualfitclub.com. https://spiritualfitclub.com/spiritual-activities-self-care-begin-today/

Staff, D. P. S. (2020, September 25). *7 Ways to Remove Toxic People From*

REFERENCES

Your Life. Dps-Site. https://www.delawarepsychologicalservices.com/post/7-ways-to-remove-toxic-people-from-your-life

The Family Institute. (n.d.). *5 Self-Care Tips for Black Women's Mental Health*. Family Institute. Retrieved March 19, 2023, from https://www.family-institute.org/behavioral-health-resources/5-self-care-tips-black-womens-mental-health

The Wilson Organisation. (2021, January 22). 12 Ways to Continue Supporting the Black Community — TWO. The Wilson Organization. https://wilsonorganization.com/12-ways-to-continue-supporting-the-black-community/

Thompson, L., & Crowley, K. (2023, January 23). *How I learned about the power of rest for Black women*. Fortune. https://fortune.com/2023/01/23/how-i-learned-about-the-power-of-rest-for-black-women/

Time Magazine. (n.d.). *6 Tips to Build a Better Bedtime Routine*. Time. https://time.com/4366736/6-tips-for-bedtime-routine/

www.ingramcontent.com/pod-product-compliance
Lightning Source LLC
Chambersburg PA
CBHW071454080526
44587CB00014B/2102